BEAD & BUTTON,
RIBBON & FELT JEWELLERY

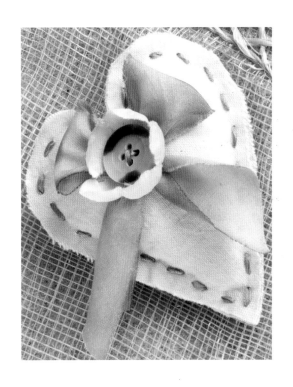

BEAD & BUTTON, RIBBON & FELT JEWELLERY

35 sewing-box treasures to make & give

DEBORAH SCHNEEBELI-MORRELL

CICO BOOKS
LONDON NEW YORK

For my two grandmothers, Ada and Dorothy,
both talented needlewomen

First published in 2007 by Cico Books
an imprint of Ryland, Peters & Small Ltd
20–21 Jockey's Fields
London WC1R 4BW

10 9 8 7 6 5 4 3 2 1

A CIP catalogue record for this book is available from the
British Library.

ISBN-10: 1 904991 66 1
ISBN-13: 978 1 904991 66 3

Printed in China

Editor: Gillian Haslam
Designer: Janet James
Illustrator: Kate Simunek
Photographer: Heini Schneebeli
Stylist: Deborah Schneebeli-Morrell

contents

Introduction

The concept of jewellery is changing as people move away from the traditional idea that only semi-precious stones can be classified as proper jewellery. Anything goes, and the trend is inventive and flamboyant. It is as if there has been an explosion of ideas, a borrowing of techniques, a reference to other cultures and a re-invention of the very term 'jewellery'!

Look around you, in clothes shops as well as in specialist outlets, in magazines and fashion photos, and study the jewellery worn by other people. You will see extraordinary combinations with all kinds of fabric and trimmings used as an integral part of the jewellery. The good thing about making jewellery from a variety of everyday materials is that these fabrics, ribbons, buttons and braids are so readily available. In fact, they may even have been collected over the years just because small scraps, often with great patterns, colours, textures and, not least, memories may be hard to throw away. Making jewellery in this way, with these modest materials, is somehow an extension of the principles of patchwork – to waste nothing and to transform, with patience and skill, an ordinary everyday material into something useful and beautiful.

To this end, never throw away a worn-out sweater if you like the colour – wash it on a very hot cycle in the washing machine to felt it. It makes an excellent material to work with and is particularly attractive when appliquéd and embroidered with a fine silk or chenille ribbon. Simpler patterned cottons can cut into circles, sewn into little pouches which can be stuffed with wadding and made into beads, or constructed into a patchwork decorated with buttons. It is most likely that a large proportion of people own a button box – these are tantalisingly interesting, often innocently containing a history or story of those family members from the past who have worn the buttons. Buttons were never thrown away, nor should they be. With the help of the ideas in this book you will develop a new respect for the innocent button and its creative potential.

Most women of a certain age will remember having a drawer full of ribbons, which were usually woven into the obligatory plait and tied in a bow – a kind of school uniform! With a child's eye you may have been aware of the colour, pattern and texture of the myriad choice available. Tartan ribbon is always a favourite, but you can also find dainty ribbons printed or woven with floral patterns. However, ribbon and braid have a nobler history too, as exquisite examples adorned the clothes of the most rich and influential and medals for the armed forces are suspended from a pretty rainbow row of satin ribbon denoting rank or honour. It is hard not to become carried away when visiting a ribbon and trimmings emporium, as a good one will have examples of silk or felt flowers, net or ruched taffeta, braid or colourful rows of cotton pompoms. All these are potential materials for your textile-inspired jewellery as they can be threaded with beads, woven through buttons or knotted to ribbons.

More conventional jewellery-making techniques and materials can be used in combination with the more unconventional use of textiles and trimmings. You may need to use an endpin to suspend a pretty bead from a ribbon or a jump ring to add a charm to a bracelet, but these well-known techniques are enhanced with the addition of a ribbon or button here and there. Another advantage is that the more usual forms of closing a necklace or bracelet can be replaced by a judicious and decorative tie of a ribbon or the knotting of a thread or cord. A button or bead and ribbon loop also makes an excellent fastening.

This extensive book explains in four inspiring chapters how to make a selection of stunning jewellery. Whilst making the pieces, your own imagination will be provoked, you will have your own ideas and develop a sense of colour, and I hope you will go on to experiment with exciting new designs of your own. There are no rules – a little patience, a modicum of skill and a burning desire to make something yourself instead of always buying it are all that is needed.

1

from the sewing box

Most people possess a sewing box full of buttons, threads and scraps of fabric. Some of us create patchwork or do a form of embroidery, crochet or knitting. All these activities provide leftover materials and scraps that we store for future projects. Sometimes small pieces of fabric such as old lace are too pretty to discard, while small samples of crochet can often be found lurking at the bottom of the box. Others are lucky enough to have inherited a sewing box with altogether more interesting objects hidden within – pearl buttons, threads and braids and perhaps fabric with vintage patterns. All these can be useful and decorative elements to create fashionable and original jewellery with textiles.

Patchwork Circle Necklace

In this project a traditional decorative patchwork technique has been reworked to provide unusual elements in this fashionable necklace. Pretty printed fabric circles with complementary patterns are gathered into little 'parcels', while the addition of decorative buttons to both sides hides the sewing stitches and gives a neat fixing for threading the copper wire which, in turn, attaches the circles to the fine copper chain. The combination of sewing and jewellery techniques can produce some really interesting pieces of jewellery.

MATERIALS

5 circles of pink fabric in different patterns, each 9cm (3½in) in diameter

Needle and strong thread

5 assorted buttons to complement the fabric, each approximately 2.5cm (1in) in diameter

10 smaller assorted buttons, approximately 1.5cm (¾in) in diameter

Jeweller's copper wire, 0.6mm or 0.8mm thickness

Double link copper chain, 45cm (18in) long

2 copper jump rings, 8mm (⅜in) in diameter

Copper lobster clasp

Wirecutters

Round-nosed pliers

Flat-nosed pliers

Scissors

1 Sew a neat running stitch around the outer edge of the fabric circles using the needle and thread.

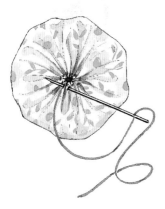

2 Pull the thread to gather the edge of the circle tightly together. Make a few holding stitches to secure the gathers and cut off the remaining thread.

3 Place a large button over the gathered centre of the circle and hold a smaller button on the back. Thread a 12.5cm (5in) length of copper wire through one of the holes in the front button, push it through the fabric and out through one of the holes in the back button. Fold the wire against the fabric and thread each end through a hole in another small button.

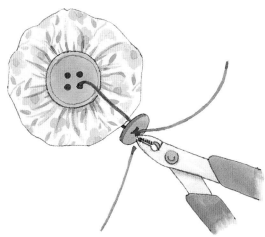

4 Push the button down to touch the edge of the fabric circle. Twist the wire tightly together, then cut off one of the ends close to the twist using the wirecutters.

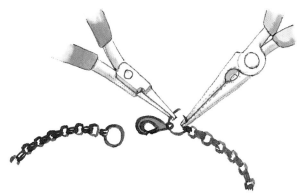

5 Secure a jump ring at each end of the copper chain, attaching a lobster clasp to one side before closing the jump ring using the two pairs of pliers.

6 Attach the circles to the central part of the chain 5cm (2in) apart by looping the long end of the wire through a chain link. Turn the wire back on itself and twist around to secure. Cut off the excess with wirecutters.

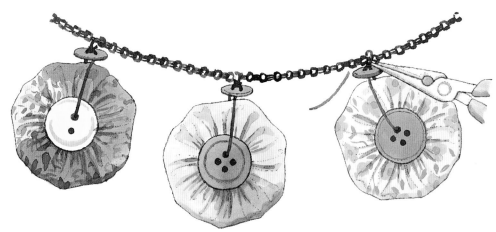

Patchwork corsage

This original corsage has been made using the same technique, although here the buttons have been attached using copper wire threaded with tiny matching seed beads and then passed through the button holes, to resemble flower stamens. The wires are twisted together on the back and the three flowers attached to a brooch pin.

Purple Felted Necklace

This striking necklace is made from a collection of black and white beads and fabric squares cut from an old felted blanket which has been dyed a rich purple. They have all been threaded onto a waxed cotton thread long enough to go over your head. The thread has been closed with a knot hidden in between the wool squares, so there is no need for a clasp. The beads are an assortment either left over from other projects or unthreaded flea-market finds. A few white buttons from the bottom of the family button box have been added to act as spacers between the beads. Like many of the projects in this book, this technique can be adapted using a variety of different materials and colours to create unique pieces of unusual jewellery.

1 Cut the felted wool into approximately 70 squares, each measuring 2 x 2cm (³⁄₄in x ³⁄₄in).

MATERIALS

Purple felted wool (an old dyed woollen blanket was used here)

1m (1 yard) waxed black thread

Collection of black and white beads and buttons in a variety of shapes, sizes and materials

Needle

Scissors

Ruler

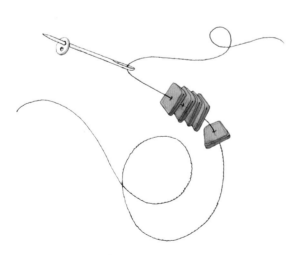

2 Thread the needle with the waxed thread and push it though the centre of five felted wool squares, then follow with a white button.

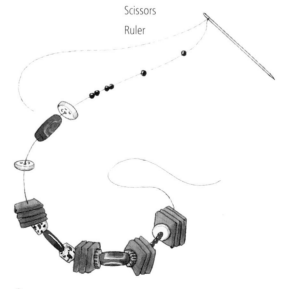

3 Continue threading more groups of beads and buttons, followed by more squares of wool, in a random design, finishing with woollen squares.

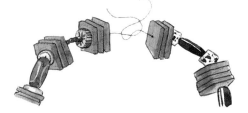

4 When the necklace has reached the required length, pull the thread taut and tie the two ends in a secure double knot. Cut off the excess thread and hide the two short ends between the squares of wool.

Indian bead bracelets

Coloured felt pieces need to be partnered with equally striking beads. The felted blanket in a muted shade of duck egg blue looks particularly good with the antique striped Indian beads, while the deep purple and soft lilac felt used on this other bracelet are complemented by spotted glass beads. Both of these strikingly modern bracelets have been simply threaded onto thick beading elastic, with the ends secured by a crimp tube.

Stuffed Fabric Bead Bracelet

A perfect patchwork project! This method of creating beads originated in the Indian subcontinent and is a highly decorative technique requiring only the simplest of sewing skills. You can make any style of bead depending on the fabric you have – you can use plain or patterned cotton, exotic silks or luxurious satins. If you are hesitating about taking a much-loved but rather worn dress to the charity shop, think again. Why not turn it into a special necklace? You could even intersperse the beads you have made with buttons from another favourite garment.

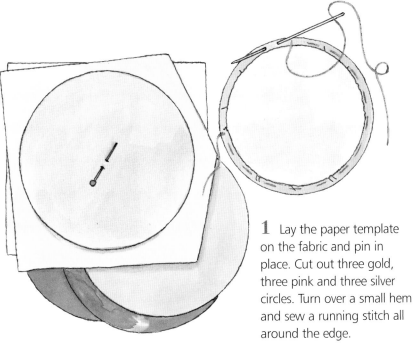

MATERIALS

Circular paper template, 6cm (2½in) in diameter
Scraps of shiny fabric, in gold, pink and silver
9 glass pearls, 2mm (¹⁄₁₆in) in diameter
1 crimp tube, 3mm (⅛in)
Pins
Needle
Strong thread, in colours to match the fabric
Cotton or polyester wadding
Beading elastic
Pencil
Needle with large eye
Scissors
Flat-nosed pliers

1 Lay the paper template on the fabric and pin in place. Cut out three gold, three pink and three silver circles. Turn over a small hem and sew a running stitch all around the edge.

2 Pull the thread gently to make the circle into a little pouch, leaving the central hole slightly open. Stuff the pouch with enough wadding to make a round bead (it helps to use a pencil to push the wadding in place).

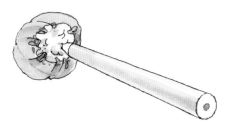

3 When the bead is stuffed tightly, pull the thread to close the opening. Oversew for a few stitches, bringing the edges together to secure, and cut off the thread. Make up all the beads in this manner.

4 Cut a 50cm (20in) length of beading elastic and thread through the needle with the large eye. You may have to flatten the end of the elastic between your fingers to make it fit through the eye of the needle. Push the needle through the centre of the stuffed beads and thread them alternately with the glass pearls. When all beads and pearls are in place, thread the elastic ends through opposite ends of the crimp tube, pull to tighten the bracelet and press the crimp with the flat-nosed pliers. Cut off the excess elastic.

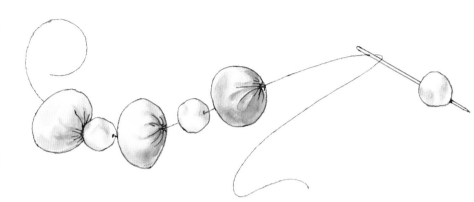

TIP

In step 4, you will probably have to unthread the needle each time you thread a pearl in place as the central hole will not be large enough to take both needle and elastic.

Fabric bead necklace

If you want to make a more everyday
necklace using the same technique, use
patterned pieces of cotton. It takes
some time to sew the beads, so if you
want to make a longer necklace add
some matching wooden beads which
are a similar size to the fabric version.
The pale blue ones used here started
off as natural wood colour but have
been immersed in a cold-water dye
bath for 30 minutes to reach the
desired tone. As with the bracelet, they
can be threaded onto beading elastic,
which gives them the advantage of
being able to stretch around the neck.
For a longer piece of jewellery, it is
probably best to thread the beads
on a waxed linen thread and tie
a secure knot to close.

Chenille Tassels with Serpentine Beads

These gorgeous chenille tassels can be purchased from good sewing or haberdashery shops – they are often used to adorn cushions, curtains, lampshades and other home decorating projects. They are so tactile and work beautifully with other materials when incorporated into imaginative jewellery designs. The subtle shades of rust brown and pea green are complementary and blend stunningly with the natural tones of the jade and serpentine beads. The necklace is long enough to fit over the head and is threaded on beading elastic, avoiding the need for any fastening.

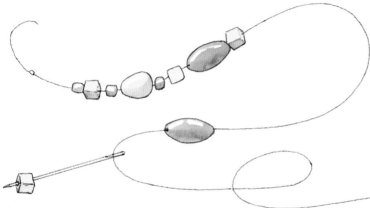

MATERIALS

9 small green seed beads, 3mm (¹⁄₈in) in diameter

30 small lemon jade cubes

5 teardrop jade beads, 6mm (¹⁄₄in) in diameter

24 elongated serpentine beads, 1.5cm (⁵⁄₈in) in diameter

2 gold-coloured crimp tubes, 2mm (¹⁄₁₆in) in diameter

2 green chenille tassels

1 rust chenille tassel

1m (1 yard) clear beading elastic, 0.5mm thick

Chenille needle (with an eye large enough to take the elastic, but small enough to fit through the smallest bead when threaded)

Scissors

Flat-nosed pliers

1 Thread the elastic through the needle. Fix a precautionary crimp bead to one end of the elastic to stop the threaded beads falling off. Thread on a seed bead, followed by a lemon jade cube, another seed bead and then a teardrop jade bead and a seed bead. Thread on another jade cube, then an elongated serpentine bead. Continue threading the serpentine and jade cubes alternately until ten serpentine beads are in place, finishing with a cube.

2 After the last cube, add a green seed bead, followed by a teardrop jade bead. Push the needle through the top of the green tassel and bring the elastic back on itself through the same teardrop bead, followed once more by the seed bead. Open out the elastic and add a jade cube. Continue with two serpentine beads, ending once more with a cube.

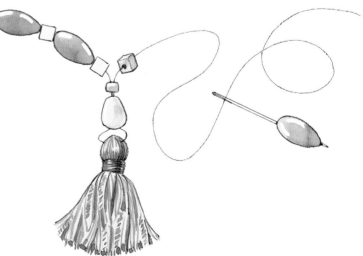

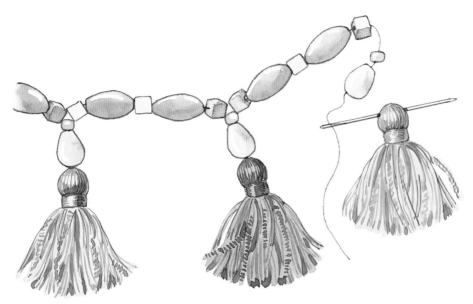

3 Continue by adding the rust tassel in the same way, followed by the second green one, until all three tassels are in place, with the rust one flanked by the two green.

4 Thread the remaining beads in exactly the same way as at the beginning of the necklace. Cut off the temporary crimp tube and thread the two ends of the elastic through the new crimp tube and press to secure with flat-nosed pliers. Cut off the elastic ends leaving 1cm (½in) and hide the ends in the adjacent beads.

Jasper and amethyst bracelet

Once you start to work with semi-precious stones, you will marvel at the stunning variety of colour, texture and form in the stones extracted from the earth and rock beneath us. These stones form some of the most ancient beads. This unusual little bracelet, using jasper and amethyst beads, is made in the same way as the main project. The beads are subtly complemented with a mauve tassel.

Antique Lace Necklace

Using dressmaking interfacing and iron-on adhesive in this necklace has eliminated the need for any stitching. The intriguing lace circles are easy to make – the lace is bonded to a stiffening fabric with an iron-on, double-sided adhesive. The lace becomes stronger, more durable and will not unravel or fray. The combination of the textured lace and plain white plastic beads threaded on black-and-white chequered ribbon makes a bold and striking necklace. Use the same techniques with different fabrics, colours or textures to create stunning, varied effects.

1 Following the manufacturer's instructions on the packaging, iron the double-sided adhesive (paper side up) to the wrong side of the lace square.

MATERIALS

Iron-on, double-sided dressmaking adhesive

Antique lace, 30 x 30cm (12 x 12in)

Thick interfacing, 30 x 15cm (12 x 6in)

3m (3 yards) of black-and-white chequered ribbon, 1cm (1/2in) wide

13 white plastic beads, 2cm (3/4in) in diameter

Iron

Light-coloured felt pen

Scissors

Hole punch

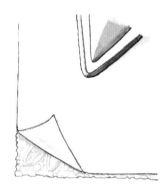

2 When the adhesive has cooled, cut the lace in half and remove the paper backing from the adhesive side of each piece of lace. Turn the lace adhesive side down, place on top of the interfacing and iron. Turn the interfacing over and iron the other piece of lace to the reverse side, creating a sandwich of lace-interfacing-lace. Do make sure that the right side of the lace faces outwards.

TIP

If you make the necklace longer, it will fit over your head and you will not need to make the fastening.

3 Using a circular item with a 4cm (1 1/2in) diameter (such as the lid of a spice jar), draw around it on to the lace using a light-coloured felt pen. Repeat to make 11 circles in total. Using sharp scissors, carefully cut out the circles just inside the pen outlines.

4 Use the hole punch to create a hole in each circle – you will need to press very firmly to make neat hole.

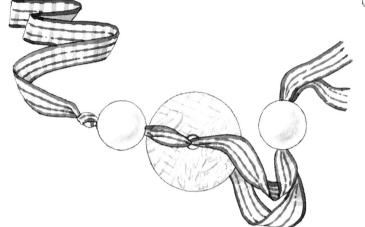

5 Cut the ribbon in half and lay the two lengths alongside each other. Tie a knot 20cm (8in) from one end of the double ribbon. Thread on a white bead, then open up the ribbon and thread one end over the front of the lace circle and through the central hole. Bring the other ribbon from underneath the disc and through the same hole, then pass the two ribbons over the other side of the lace circle and through the next bead.

6 Continue threading the beads and discs in this manner until all the circles and 12 white beads are in place. After the last bead, tie a knot, leave a 2cm (¾in) gap and tie a further knot. Thread on a bead and tie a knot immediately after to hold in place. This makes the fastening bead. Repeat this sequence at the other end, but omit the last bead and instead leave a 3cm (1¼in) section of ribbon and tie a final knot. This makes the hole to enclose the bead at the other end.

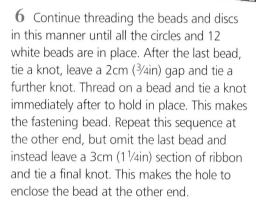

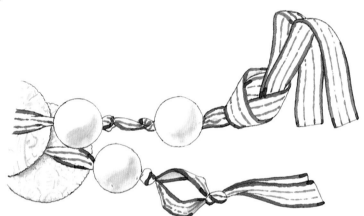

Lace disc earrings on wavy braid

The lace discs are threaded in the same way
as the necklace, but beads have been
substituted for the buttons and the ribbon
has been replaced by a wavy antique braid.
This method of stringing lace discs, beads,
buttons and ribbon together would make
a stylish, modern belt.

Cameo Lace Brooch

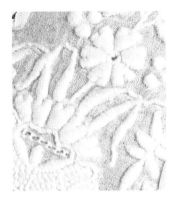

This is an elegant and inventive variation on the classic cameo brooch, created entirely from fabric and using iron-on, double-sided dressmaking adhesive. The bonding technique extends the life of the antique lace which may be fragile. The use of silk ribbon for the simple stitches surrounding the lace motif is a traditional embroidery technique which is easy and effective, yet strong and durable. The little parcel is stuffed with a wadding to give substance to the brooch. These sewing techniques are well worth exploring and would suit small bags or a spectacle case.

MATERIALS

Iron-on, double-sided dressmaking adhesive

Antique lace, approximately 7 x 9cm (2¾ x 3½in)

2 pieces of linen in indigo and natural colour,
  each 10 x 12cm (4 x 4¾in)

1.5m (1½ yards) pale blue silk ribbon, 3mm (⅛in) wide

Cotton or polyester wadding

Scissors

Needle with long eye to take silk ribbon

Pencil

Brooch pin

1 Cut the dressmaking adhesive to the same size as the lace. Position the lace face side down, place the adhesive on top (paper side uppermost) and iron on to the back of the lace using a medium-hot iron. It is always best to follow the manufacturer's instructions on the packaging. Cut out an oval shape from the lace with the paper backing still in place. The oval should be approximately 7cm (2¾in) high and 5cm (2½in) wide. Peel off the backing paper and place the lace adhesive side down, right side of the lace facing up, centrally onto the natural linen square. Iron again to bond the lace to the linen.

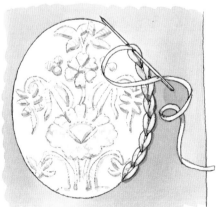

2 Thread the needle with the narrow silk ribbon and sew a chain stitch border all around the outer edge of the oval lace shape.

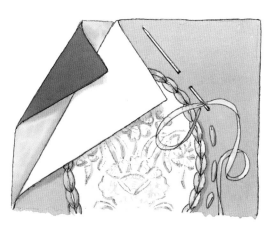

3 Place the linen with the lace oval over the indigo linen. Sew a line of running stitch through the two layers of linen 1cm (½in) away from the chain stitch border, leaving a 4cm (1½in) gap on one side.

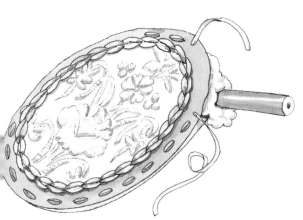

4 Cut through the two layers of linen 5mm (¼in) from the running stitch. Push the wadding between the layers so it makes a shallow pad. It helps to use a pencil so you can distribute the wadding evenly inside the pouch. Continue the running stitches to close the gap. Hide the ribbon end between the linen layers. Turn the pouch over and sew the brooch pin into place on the back, using the ribbon. Place it just above the centre.

Crochet Circles on Silk Ribbon

Crochet is making a comeback, and it's about time too – it's a wonderful decorative technique which is as easy as knitting. If you rummage around in linen baskets in flea markets, you will most probably find small examples of crocheted flowers – they seem to be the first thing people make when they learn to crochet. The crochet circles used here were discovered in my sewing box, left over from another project. They have been perfectly matched with the crochet-covered beads which can be found in a good bead shop and the two strands of exquisite hand-dyed silk ribbon. This is a quick project to create, and if you enjoy making the necklace, why not learn to crochet and create your own designs and colourways?

MATERIALS

5 small crochet circles, in orange and pale and deep pinks, approximately 3cm (1¼in) in diameter

4 large crochet circles, in the same colours, approximately 5cm (2in) in diameter

4 crochet-covered beads in pink and two-toned pink stripes, 2.5cm (1in) in diameter

2m (2 yards) yellow/red hand-dyed silk ribbon, 1cm (½in) wide

2m (2 yards) pink hand-dyed silk ribbon, 2.5cm (1in) wide

Crochet hook

Scissors

1 Lay the two lengths of ribbon alongside each other and tie them together in a single knot 20cm (8in) from one end. Thread the narrower yellow/red ribbon over the front of the smaller orange crochet circle, then pull it through the central hole from behind with the help of the crochet hook. Bring the wider pink ribbon through the same hole from behind in the same manner.

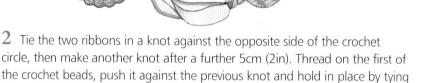

2 Tie the two ribbons in a knot against the opposite side of the crochet circle, then make another knot after a further 5cm (2in). Thread on the first of the crochet beads, push it against the previous knot and hold in place by tying a similar knot on the other side of the bead.

3 Leave another gap of 5cm (2in) after the bead and tie another knot, then thread the ribbons through the larger pink crochet circle in exactly the same manner as the first one. Always use the crochet hook to pull the ribbons through from each side.

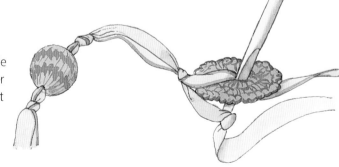

4 Tie a knot tightly against the pink circle and continue threading the ribbons, beads and remaining crochet circles. Vary the order of colour and the length of ribbon between the knots. When all four beads, three small crochet circles and the remaining large ones are in place, tie a knot, leave a further 5cm (2in), then tie another knot. Feed the two ribbon ends through the last small crochet circle; repeat at the other end threading the ribbons through from the other side. Knot the two ribbon lengths coming through from each side and cut off the ribbon ends, leaving 1.5cm (³/4in) tails.

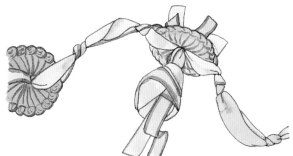

Ruched Net Trim
with Pink Shell Fragments

This is an incredibly simple way to decorate a plain cashmere sweater. The soft, three-tone gathered net trim was purchased from a specialist ribbon and trimmings emporium. The trim is already gathered on elastic and is fixed to the edge of the neckline through small shell fragments with narrow pale pink silk ribbons. The pretty dyed shells are added evenly around the trim. The advantage of attaching the net in this way is both its simplicity and the fact that it is so quick to remove, giving you two garments for the price of one.

MATERIALS

Sweater of your choice

Three-tone soft net trimming, long enough to reach around the neck of the sweater (approximately 80cm/32in)

18 small, pink-dyed shell fragments

1m (1 yard) pale pink ribbon, 4mm (^{3}/16in) wide

Dressmaking pins

Scissors

Needle with eye large enough to take ribbon

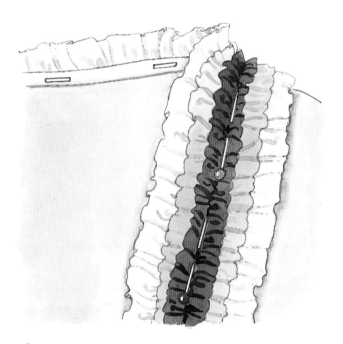

1 Pin the net trim all around the neck of the sweater along the centre of the darker net. Make sure that it sits neatly above the rib edging on the neck. At the point where both ends of the trim meet, overlap slightly and cut off the excess length.

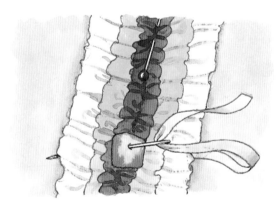

2 Thread the needle with the narrow pink ribbon and sew a shell fragment in place centrally in the net trim. Leave a 5cm (2in) tail of ribbon without a knot showing on the front.

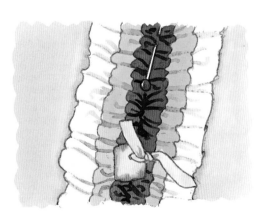

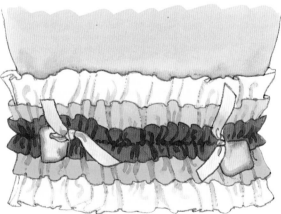

3 Bring the ribbon back through the sweater just by the edge of the shell and tie tightly into a double knot with the tail left on the front. Cut off the ribbon ends to leave tails of 2cm (¾in).

4 Continue sewing the shells in place, 4cm (1½in) apart, in the same manner all around the neck of the sweater. You may like to decorate the end of the sleeves in a similar fashion.

Gathered choker

This sophisticated grey, gathered trim is probably intended to be used in upholstery or costume making. Here, however, it makes a beautiful choker with two identical faceted metallic buttons used for decoration, one to fasten at the back and one to embellish the front.

Wool and Ribbon Flower Plait

This double-rosette flower is cleverly made from the ribbed cuffs of worn-out woollen sweaters, but unlike the green leaves and stamens they have not been felted. The flower has been attached to the ends of a neat plait made from two ribbons and a strip of knitted wool. Plaiting fabrics in this way is a technique borrowed from plaited and rag-rug makers. It produces a strong and durable fabric that can be made highly decorative by weaving different colours, textures and materials alongside each other.

MATERIALS

1m (1 yard) blue-red shot rayon ribbon, 8mm (³/₈in) wide

1m (1 yard) olive green silk ribbon, 8mm (³/₈in) wide

1m (1 yard) mauve knitted fabric cut from an old sweater, 8mm (³/₈in) wide

Cuff from pale blue sweater

Cuff from mauve sweater

Scraps of green-brown felted wool

30cm (12in) of mauve silk ribbon, 4mm (³/₁₆in) wide

Scissors

Needle

Grey thread

1 Take the blue-red and green ribbons and the strip of mauve knitted fabric and plait tightly together. Sew a couple of holding stitches 3cm (1¹/₄in) from each end.

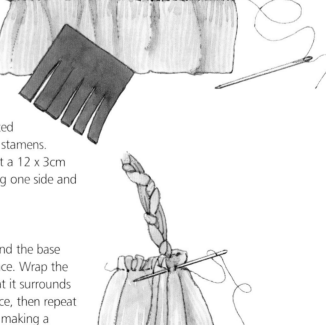

2 Cut a 3 x 3cm (1¹/₄ x 1¹/₄in) square of felted green-brown wool and cut one side into five stamens. Leave 1cm (¹/₂in) uncut on the other side. Cut a 12 x 3cm (4³/₄ x 1¹/₄in) length of blue cuff, gather along one side and pull tightly to draw together.

TIP

This project provides a great way to re-use favourite but well-worn sweaters.

3 Wrap the stamens around the base of the plait and stitch in place. Wrap the gathered cuff on top so that it surrounds the plait, stitch firmly in place, then repeat on the other end, this time making a second gathered cuff from the mauve cuff.

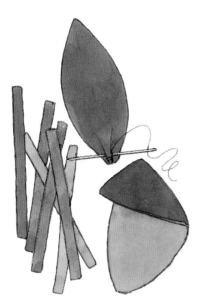

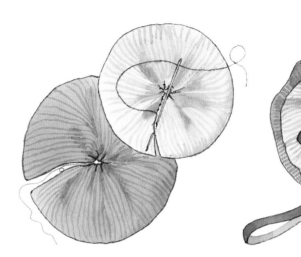

4 Cut out two leaf shapes 9cm (3½in) long from the felted green-brown wool. Stitch them at the base to make three-dimensional leaf shapes. Cut out six narrow strips 6cm (2½in) long from the same wool to make stamens.

5 Cut out a 20 x 3cm (8 x 1¼in) strip of the blue cuff. Gather one side and pull tightly into a rosette, then sew up the open side. Cut out a slightly larger mauve cuff, 25 x 3.5cm (10 x 1⅜in). Gather to make a second rosette and sew up the open side as before.

6 Place the blue rosette inside the larger mauve rosette. Fold each stamen in half and push the two ends through the gathered hole at the base of the two rosettes. Pull the ends through at the base and sew together to secure. Cut of the protruding stamen ends.

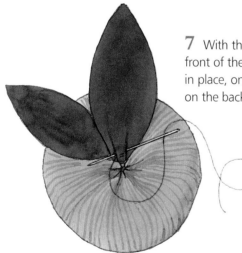

7 With the green side facing the front of the flower, stitch the leaves in place, one slightly overlapping on the back of the rosette.

8 Bring the two ends of the plait over the back of the flower, making one slightly longer than the other. Thread the needle with the narrow mauve silk ribbon and sew and tie the flower onto each plait in two places.

Felted wool butterfly brooch with plaited body

This charming butterfly brooch is quick and enjoyable to make. The simple butterfly shape has been decorated with appliqué wool which has been embroidered with coloured silk ribbon, and a plaited body has been made from woollen strips woven with a thick pink chenille thread. The jolly colours make it a perfect present for a young child.

Pearl-buttoned Woollen Cuff

Here's another stylish use for a favourite worn-out sweater – make two of these fashionable cuffs to keep your wrists warm and decorated in the winter. The sweater has been felted by washing it on the hottest machine wash. The designer sweater used here was unusually bonded with green and brown wool on either side, and the chenille embroidery works particularly well with the texture and colour of the wool. A neat chain stitch on one side of the fabric creates a simple running stitch on the reverse. The assorted pearl buttons are held in place with decorative ribbon ties on the back. If you prefer a plainer look, you could fasten the cuff with a transparent press stud.

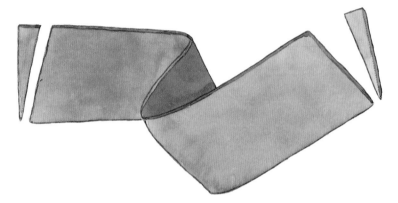

MATERIALS

Felted wool

7 pearl buttons in varying sizes

50cm (20in) pale pink silk ribbon, 4mm (^{3}/$_{16}$in) wide

1m (1 yard) deep pink, hand-dyed bias silk ribbon, 1.5cm (^{3}/$_4$in) wide

Green chenille thread

Chenille needle

Needle with a long eye for silk ribbon

Scissors

1 Cut a rectangle measuring 22 x 4cm (8^1/$_2$ x 1^1/$_2$ in) from the felted wool. Cut out a wedge measuring 5mm (^{1}/$_4$in) from each end at the base, cutting at an angle to nothing. This creates one long side 1cm (^{1}/$_2$in) longer than its opposite side.

2 Thread the chenille needle with the chenille thread and stitch a row of chain stitch all around the cuff on the green side 5mm (^{1}/$_4$in) in from the edge.

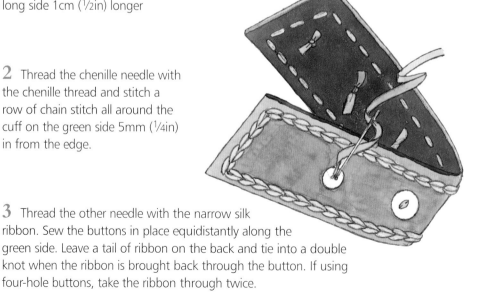

3 Thread the other needle with the narrow silk ribbon. Sew the buttons in place equidistantly along the green side. Leave a tail of ribbon on the back and tie into a double knot when the ribbon is brought back through the button. If using four-hole buttons, take the ribbon through twice.

4 Cut the wider silk ribbon in half and sew one length into the wool halfway down the short side. Don't take the ribbon through to the front – the wool should be thick enough to hide the stitch. Pull the ribbon through to have two equal lengths. Repeat on the other end.

2 ribbons and flowers

One of the most enjoyable activities for a craftsperson is to visit a ribbon and trimmings emporium – you will be amazed at the extent and quality of what is available as there has been a real revival in the use of trimmings, felt flowers, ribbons, cords and braid. In earlier times, when women wore hats and clothes were more formal, the use of such trimmings was widespread and there was a vibrant industry making these intriguing items. Today we can still find satin, silk, taffeta and chiffon ribbons, hand- and dip-dyed, woven and printed, wired and ruched. Some of the most inspiring examples of trimmings are the lovely felt or chiffon flowers, bunches of stamens and small posies of silk flowers. All these can be cleverly combined with other elements to create truly original pieces of jewellery.

Ribbon Choker with Velvet Flowers

This charming ribbon choker has been cleverly decorated with velvet flowers which have been attached using a pretty rayon ribbon. No sewing skills are required for this project even though nearly all the elements are fabric. Some specialist ribbon suppliers sell an inspiring array of fabric flowers which were traditionally used for hat decoration or for corsages. When choosing all the elements for your design, think carefully about the colour, tone and texture of the different materials as this will help you to achieve a professional-looking finished article.

MATERIALS

40cm (16in) length of purple rayon ribbon, 1cm (½in) wide

40cm (16in) length of dip-dyed orange taffeta ribbon, 3cm (1¼in) wide

6 burnt orange velvet flowers, 2cm (¾in) in diameter

Knitting needle

2 gold-coloured box calottes

2 gold-coloured jump rings, 7mm (⅜in) and 5mm (¼in) in diameter

1 gold-coloured lobster clasp

Scissors

Flat-nosed pliers

Round-nosed pliers

1 Cut a 6cm (2½in) length of the purple rayon ribbon and tie it to the orange ribbon approximately 6cm (2½in) from one end. Bring the two ends of the purple ribbon through the back of the velvet flower (use the point of a knitting needle to help to push them through).

2 Turn the flower around so that it is in the correct position and tie the purple ribbon in a single tight knot to secure. Cut the ends off neatly, allowing them to project slightly over the petals of the flower.

3 Continue adding the flowers in the same manner until you have all six flowers in place. Make sure you leave 5cm (2in) of ribbon free at each end.

4 Push each end of the orange ribbon into a box calotte and close very tightly, using the flat-nosed pliers. Attach the two jump rings to the rings on the calottes and finish by attaching the lobster clasp to the larger jump ring.

Button choker

This button choker is made by threading a wire-edged pale pink organdie ribbon through smoky toned mother-of-pearl buttons. As with the orange taffeta ribbon choker, the ribbon ends are securely held in small box calottes. If you wish, add a touch of glue to the ribbon ends for extra security.

Chiffon Ribbon and Glass Bead Necklace

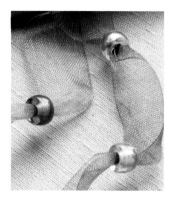

This effective but simple project is very easy to make. The shot green and bronze chiffon ribbons complement the foil-lined glass beads so well. The central hole in the bead needs to be just large enough to pass the threaded needle through, but narrow enough to hold the ribbon securely in place. Too large a hole means the beads slide out of place; too narrow and the needle will not pass through. The gold toggle clasp, which picks up the colour of the ribbon, is a simple way of finishing the necklace and works particularly well with ribbon.

MATERIALS

Needle

70cm (28in) lengths of chiffon ribbon in blue-bronze and green-bronze, 1cm ($\frac{1}{2}$in) wide

11 pale green foil-lined glass beads with a 3mm ($\frac{1}{8}$in) diameter hole

10 smaller green foil-lined glass beads with a 3mm ($\frac{1}{8}$in) diameter hole

2 turquoise foil-lined glass beads with a 5mm ($\frac{1}{4}$in) diameter hole

Gold-coloured toggle clasp, 8mm ($\frac{1}{8}$in)

Beading glue

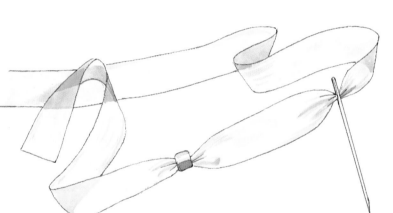

1 Thread the needle with the blue-bronze ribbon and thread the first pale green bead along the ribbon 10cm (4in) from one end.

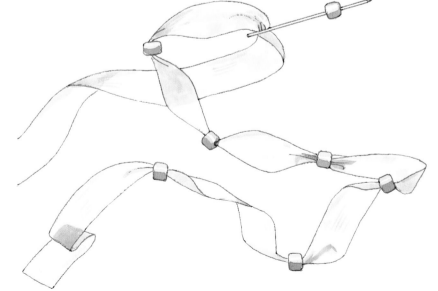

2 Continue threading the beads, leaving a gap of approximately 4cm (1$\frac{1}{2}$in) between beads until eleven beads are in place. Lay to one side.

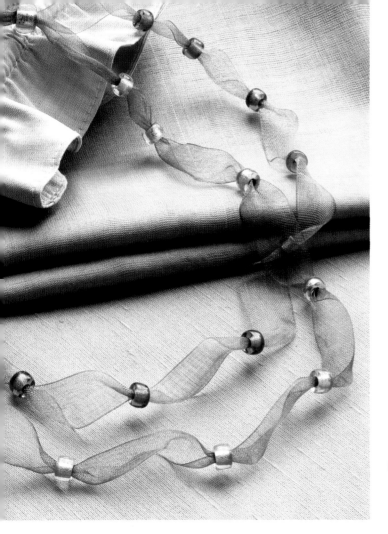

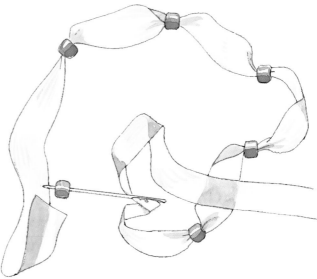

3 Take the green-bronze length of ribbon and thread in a similar manner with ten green beads.

4 Bring the two bead-threaded ribbons together and pass them both through a larger turquoise bead. Then pass these two ribbon ends through the ring on one side of the clasp.

5 Bring the double ribbon back on itself and tie into a knot. Repeat with the other two remaining ends, this time adding the toggle.

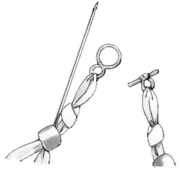

6 Using a needle, carefully dab some beading glue into the large bead and push the ribbon ends into the bead. When the glue sets, the ribbon will stay in place.

Dip-dyed chiffon ribbon threaded with large beads

If you want to use larger beads, they must be light in weight as heavier glass ones will drag on the ribbon when worn. The pretty faceted vintage plastic beads used here are ideal. A wider ribbon has been used, as the central hole in the bead is proportionately larger. This is one of the simplest projects in this book – try using a variety of ribbons, such as chiffon, satin, velvet or taffeta, and choose beads from your collection to match. Whilst experimenting, you can make a necklace for every day of the week.

Wired Ribbon Roses on Copper Chain

Soft pink teamed with the subtle shades of natural copper makes a stylish colour combination. In this project wired taffeta ribbon in a graduated colour is easily turned into a vintage-effect old rose – simply pull the wire that runs through the edge of the ribbon to gather up one side and the ribbon adopts a classic rose shape. Adding a central bead and a sepal-like bead cap on an endpin helps to create the illusion of a charming flower. The roses hang loosely on the copper chain, interspersed with pretty pink glass leaves.

1 Cut the three ribbons in half, into two even lengths. Take one length and turn the ends of the ribbon over, sewing them neatly in place with a needle and thread. Pull the wire slightly at one end and bend it over to secure it, then pull the wire at the other end tightly, making sure you don't lose the wire protruding at the beginning.

MATERIALS

1m (1 yard) each of wired toned taffeta ribbon in three different shades of pink, 4cm (1½in) wide

Needle and thread

6 small pink glass beads

6 copper endpins

6 copper bead caps

80cm (32in) copper chain

7 pink glass leaves, approximately 2cm (¾in) long

1 copper jump ring

Round-nosed pliers

Flat-nosed pliers

Wirecutters

2 When the ribbon has been pulled tightly, turn it around on itself into a 'rose'. Sew the base together tightly as you turn and twist the protruding wires together to secure.

3 Thread a pink glass bead onto an endpin, then push the endpin through the rose from the front and out at the base. Add a bead cap to the protruding endpin.

4 Thread the endpin through a link in the chain 20cm (8in) from one end and bend it over with round-nosed pliers. Twist the loop around on itself to secure, then cut off the excess wire using the wirecutters. Add five more roses in this way, spaced 10cm (4in) apart.

5 Attach the pink glass leaves, one equidistantly between each rose and two on each side after the last roses, by closing the leaf rings tightly over the links in the copper chain.

6 Cut the excess chain 20cm (8in) from the last attached rose and join the two ends of the chain with a copper jump ring using two pairs of pliers.

Rose corsage

This blue-toned rose has been made in a similar way to the pink roses in the main project but instead of using a bead in the centre of the flower, loops of hand-dyed bias cut silk ribbon have been attached to create the effect of stamens. The leaves have been made by folding the darker side of the ribbon back on itself. The corsage has been stitched together at the back and attached to a scarf clip.

French Pressed Flower Garland

One of the easiest and quickest of all the projects in this chapter, this charming garland is perfect to wear on a sunny summer's day. The little felt flowers, which have been simply threaded on a garland of spring-green seed beads, were traditionally used in hat decoration and they are now being used with renewed interest by clothes designers and jewellers. They are supplied in small bundles from a good haberdashery shop or ribbon emporium. They can be expensive, but you will not need many for this project and any leftover can be used elsewhere.

MATERIALS

2 small silver crimp tubes, 1.3mm (¹/₁₆in)

1m (1 yard) tiger tail

Green seed beads, approximately 3mm (¹/₈in) in diameter

7 viola felt flowers, 3cm (1 ¹/₄in) in diameter

7 mauve felt daisies, 2.5cm (1in) in diameter

Flat-nosed pliers

Scissors

1 Attach a precautionary crimp tube at one end of the tiger tail. Thread approximately five green seed beads onto the tiger tail.

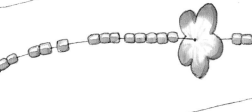

2 Next, thread on a felt flower, followed by approximately 20 more seed beads.

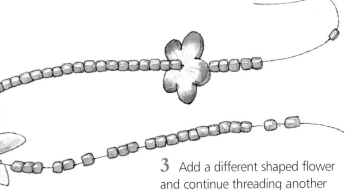

3 Add a different shaped flower and continue threading another 20 or so seed beads after it.

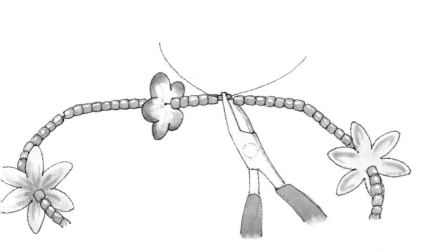

4 When 14 flowers have been threaded in place, add about 10 beads after the last flower. Cut off the precautionary crimp tube and discard. Bring the two ends of the tiger tail together through the new crimp tube, pull fairly tight (but allow the beads some room to move or the necklace will not hang properly). Press to secure with the flat-nosed pliers. Cut off the excess, leaving a small length to hide inside the adjoining seed beads.

Use any leftover flowers to make a pretty pair of matching earrings.

VARIATION

Garland of mauve delica beads

This delicate garland has been threaded on fine copper wire, giving the necklace a more irregular feel. In contrast to the main project, the larger velvet flowers are also threaded so that they lie flat against the beaded wire. This is achieved by bringing the copper wire up through the flower from behind, then through a small button and bead before it is taken back through the flower once more. The delica beads used here are tiny, metallic-effect glass seed beads.

57

Threaded Sequin Choker with Ribbon Ties

Most people are familiar with the shiny decorative quality of sequins when sewn onto fabric. This form of embellishment is often associated with the Indian subcontinent, but sequins have other decorative possibilities, as shown in this project. When threaded tightly together onto a single thread, they have a subtler appeal – you see shiny glimpses when larger sequins adjoin a group of smaller ones. As there is some spring and flexibility in a group of threaded sequins, it is easy to tie a piece of ribbon between them as they will spring back together to enclose the ribbon neatly, just leaving the ribbon tails on show.

MATERIALS

Tiger tail

3 silver crimp tubes, 1.3mm (^{1}/16in) in diameter

Selection of sequins in varying sizes and colours, such as blue, gold, bronze, purple and pink

4 fire-polished glass beads (2 faceted roundels and 2 faceted pink)

Lobster clasp

Figure-of-eight ring

60cm (24in) lengths of chiffon ribbon in bronze and blue, 1cm (^{1}/2in) wide

Scissors

Flat-nosed pliers

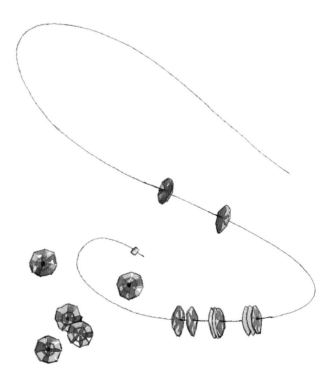

TIP

A little white glue run along the edge of the ribbon will stop it fraying. You can cut the edge again when the glue has dried for extra neatness and to ensure it is barely visible.

1 Cut a 60cm (24in) length of tiger tail and secure a precautionary crimp tube to one end (to prevent the sequins slipping off). Thread a group of identical sequins, measuring 2cm (^{3}/4in) in length, onto the tiger tail.

2 Thread another section of smaller sequins onto the tiger tail. Continue in this manner with each section in a different colour. You can vary the length of these groups slightly, but always change the size and colour as each new group is added.

3 When the sequins measure approximately 40cm (16in) in length, finish one end by adding a faceted roundel bead, followed by a crimp tube and finally a small pink bead. Continue by threading the tiger tail through the hole in the lobster clasp, then take it back on itself through the pink bead and the crimp tube. Pull to tighten and press the crimp tube with the flat-nosed pliers to secure. Cut off the excess tiger tail, leaving a small length to hide inside the roundel bead.

4 Cut off the temporary crimp tube and thread the beads and crimp in exactly the same way as at the other end, but this time attaching the figure-of-eight ring. Pull the tiger tail tightly and press the crimp tube to secure, hiding the end as before inside the glass roundel.

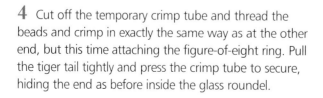

5 Cut a 12cm (4¾in) length of ribbon and fold in half, then pull the loop around the tiger tail between a group of sequins. Feed the ribbon ends back through the loop and pull tightly to secure. Adjust the sequins to enclose the knot.

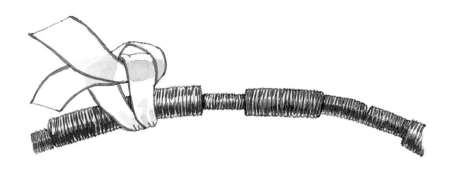

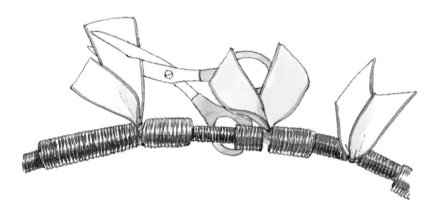

6 Continue adding the ribbon ties, using the two different colours and spacing them out approximately 5cm (2in) apart. When they are all in place, cut the edges of the ribbon on a slant with the sharp scissors, leaving tails measuring 2.5cm (1in).

Stretchy sequin bracelet with printed chiffon ties

Chiffon ribbon is available in a huge range of colours and designs, including the printed variety shown here in this pretty bead and sequin bracelet. Sequins work particularly well when used in conjunction with iridescent seed beads, creating a sparkly effect.

Chiffon Flower Necklace

Pale blue chiffon flowers float delicately along fine silk ribbon. The chiffon flowers, purchased from a ribbon supplier, come in small packs which contain a large number of petals. They are used in dressmaking as decorative accessories, but adapt beautifully as elements in this magical garland. Three layers of chiffon petals are laid on top of each other to make the flowers. A bead on an endpin holds the petals in place in front, while a bead cap and a dab of glue hold them behind the flower. Small blue glass beads are attached through simple knots in the ribbon.

MATERIALS

6 assorted blue glass beads, approximately 1cm (½in) in diameter

10 small blue glass beads, 5mm (¼in) in diameter

11 gold-coloured endpins

5 gold-coloured bead caps

15 layers of pale blue chiffon flowers

5 tiny turquoise seed beads

1m (1 yard) pale blue silk ribbon, 8mm (³⁄₈in) wide

1m (1 yard) toned olive green silk ribbon, 3mm (¹⁄₈in) wide

1 blue button with two holes, 1.5cm (³⁄₄in) in diameter
Round-nosed pliers

Flat-nosed pliers

Wirecutters

White craft glue

1 Thread an assortment of the blue glass beads onto endpins in pairs, with the larger shaped glass beads at the base. Using the round-nosed pliers, turn the excess endpin into a loop. Hold this loop with one pair of pliers and use the other pair to pull the end around on itself to make a secure twist. Cut off the excess with wirecutters. Make up six endpins in this way.

2 Thread an endpin through a turquoise seed bead, followed by a small glass bead. Follow this with the first layer of a chiffon flower, then add two more layers, adjusting the petals to make a flower. Turn the flower upside down and add a dab of glue followed by a bead cap, to secure the layers in place. Push down and turn the endpin into a loop as before. Cut off the excess wire. Make up five flowers in total.

3 Thread one flower centrally onto the two ribbons and tie the ribbons in a single knot around the loop.

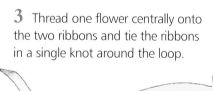

4 Add a bead cluster on each side of this first flower, then tie the double ribbon in a single knot, enclosing the loop at the top of the bead cluster approximately 7cm (2¾in) away from the flower.

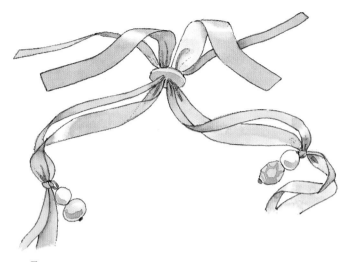

5 Add all the flowers and bead clusters in this manner, spacing them out evenly on each side of the central flower. Finish with a bead cluster (without a flower) at each end of the ribbons. Thread the double ribbons at each end through separate holes in the button, from the underside. At this stage you can adjust the length of the necklace.

6 Bring the double ribbon ends back through the opposite button holes (from the top) and tie into a double knot on the underside. Dab a spot of white glue on the knot for added security. Cut the ribbon about 2cm (¾in) from the ends, smear the cut edge with a little glue and, when dry, cut again to give a neat finish.

Chiffon flower earrings

These ultimately feminine flower drop earrings are easy to make and match the garland beautifully. The bead at the base is threaded on to an endpin, and in order to make it swing freely, it is looped around the ring at the base of an eyepin, which has been threaded with a small blue glass bead. As in the necklace, the petals are lightly glued in place and a gold-coloured bead cap follows on. Six assorted beads are threaded above the flower onto the length of the eyepin, which is itself looped around the base ring on a gold earring hook.

Suede Leaf Necklace Tie

As with the felt, velvet and chiffon flowers, these stylish suede leaves were bought from a ribbon supplier. The leaves have been attached to the olive green rayon ribbon and ivory ric rac with double silk ties, fed through a selection of pearl buttons. Adding the buttons along the length of the ribbons provides extra decoration and makes an unusual necklace. To wear, simply thread one of the end leaves between the ribbon and ric rac and pull gently so that it hangs lower than the leaf on the opposite end.

MATERIALS

Selection of silk ribbons in variety of greens,
   3mm (1/8in) wide
1.5m (1 1/2 yards) olive rayon ribbon, 1cm (1/2in) wide
1.5m (1 1/2 yards) ivory ric rac, 5mm (1/4in) wide
13 pearl buttons
Selection of six suede leaves
Small, sharp scissors
White craft glue

1 Cut the narrow silk ribbons into 8cm (3 1/4in) lengths, lay them across the rayon ribbon and ric rac and tie into a single knot, leaving 4–5cm (1 1/4–1 1/2in) of ribbon and ric rac at the end.

2 Using sharp scissors, puncture each leaf with two small slits, just large enough to accommodate the ribbons. Place a small pearl button over a leaf. Bring the silk ribbon ends through the slits and the two holes in the buttons. Tie into a single knot, add a dab of glue to the knot and tie a second knot to secure. Trim the ends of the ribbons to 1.5cm (3/4in). For extra neatness, smear a dab of glue along the trimmed edge of the ribbons and cut again when dry.

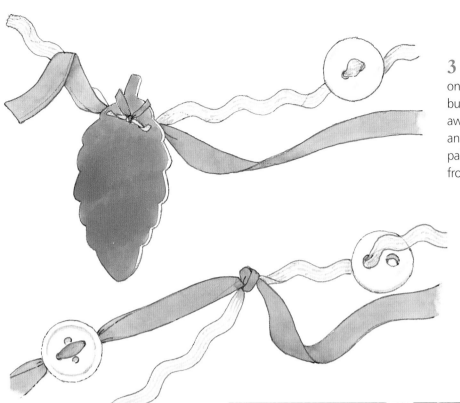

3 Thread a larger pearl button onto the ric rac from behind the button, approximately 5cm (2in) away from the first leaf. Then tie another knot enclosing the next pair of silk ribbon ties 12cm (4³⁄₄in) from the first attached leaf.

4 Continue adding leaves into knots and threading buttons alternately onto ribbon or ric rac until three leaves are in place, each 12cm (4³⁄₄in) apart. Create three more sections 12cm (4³⁄₄in) apart with no attached leaves, adding the buttons onto alternate ribbon and ric rac. This section will make up the centre of the necklace (the part that goes around the back of the neck). Add three more leaves to match the beginning and cut off the extra ribbon and ric rac leaving 5cm (2in) tails, as in step 2. Seal the edges with a dab of white glue to stop fraying.

Ribbon Rosebud Corsage

These ribbon roses in autumnal tones, framed with a rosette of satin-edged ribbon, make the perfect corsage. The ribbon used for the roses has a fine, soft wire running down each edge. Pulling one of these wires gathers the edge, while the ungathered wired edge can be arranged into ruffles and folds. Make a bold statement and wear two together or attach them to a plain silk evening bag. They would look great used to hold a silk scarf or pashmina in place, or would work well as a hair adornment, especially if the ribbon colour matches your outfit.

MATERIALS

2 x 50cm (20in) lengths of deep red-toned taffeta wired ribbon, 4cm (1½in) wide

1m (1 yard) burnt orange satin-edged ribbon, 2cm (¾in) wide

Soft jeweller's wire

2 gilded glass buttons with sewing holes on the back

Needle

Strong thread to match the ribbon tones

1m (1 yard) plum satin-edged ribbon, 2cm (¾in) wide

Brooch pin

Scissors

1 Make the two roses following the instructions on page 52, but omit the central beads and bead caps on the back. Cut a 15cm (6in) length of wire and thread halfway through the back of the glass button.

2 Fold the wire in half and twist tightly together so that the button is held securely and you have a long twisted tail.

3 Make a hole in the base of the rose with the eye end of the needle and push the wire tail on the button through this hole. Pull tightly so that the button sits snugly in the inside base of the rose.

4 Turn the rose upside down, twist the wire around and hold against the base where the wire emerges. Start to loop the plum satin-edged ribbon around the base of the flower, sewing each loop and twist of the wire in place as you go.

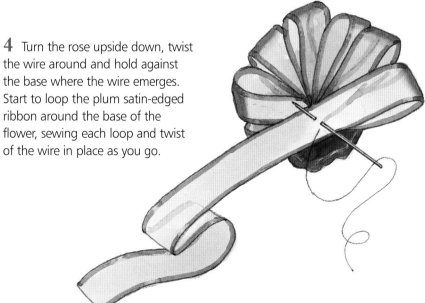

TIP

To make a larger rosette, simply choose a wider satin-edged ribbon (see the purple rosette variation on page 71 for an example of this).

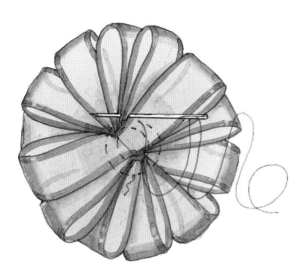 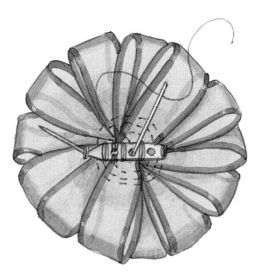

5 When all the ribbon has been looped evenly around the base of the rose, finish with a few holding stitches. The wire holding the button will be completely hidden by the ribbon folds.

6 Place the brooch pin centrally onto the back of the rosette and sew in place. Stitch first through the holes in the pin, then oversew the metal bar to make it secure. Finish off neatly and cut off the excess thread.

Purple rosette

This rather luxurious royal purple rosette is made by simply gathering one edge of the ribbon and stitching the gathered edge together to form the circle, joining the cut edges on the underside with a plain running stitch. A smaller ribbon forms the inner circle and a velvet-covered button makes a contrasting central accent.

3

beads, jewels and charms

Beads, jewels and charms are the more well-known elements in the making of jewellery. They cover a vast range of styles, design and materials. Although there are many ideas in this chapter for you to follow, once you find yourself in a good bead shop you will not fail to be tempted and inspired by the sheer volume and variety of what is available. Semi-precious stones and beads can be expensive to buy, but when used in small quantity and combined with other elements they become quite affordable. As always, it is the choice of materials and their combination that makes a good piece of jewellery. These are sensitive and important aspects of design and the projects in this chapter will assist you in learning this vital skill.

Freshwater Pearl and Polka Dot Necklace

This unusual and inventive necklace is a subtle variation on a classic pearl necklace. A long strip of the softest net has been woven between the pearls, creating a delicate transparent ruff effect. Pearls are traditionally strung on a knotted silk thread in order to prevent them rubbing against each other and causing damage to the surface. Here, weaving the net between the pearls helps to recreate this buffer, while the pearls strung tightly together on tiger tail help to keep the ruff firmly in place. When using semi-precious jewels, such as these pearls, it is best to match the quality by using solid silver findings. This simple yet effective technique can be applied to a variety of different beads and weaving materials.

MATERIALS

Pink polka dot net measuring 2m (2 yards) long and 3.5cm (1³⁄₈in) wide

Tiger tail

1 crimp tube

62 assorted smaller pink tinged pearls

32 large freshwater pearls

2 silver crimp ends with ring

1 silver snake clasp

Scissors

Flat-nosed pliers

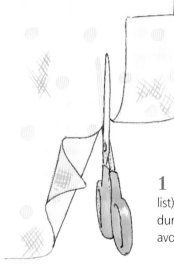

1 Cut the net to size (see Materials list). If necessary, you can join a piece during the threading process to avoid having to buy too much net.

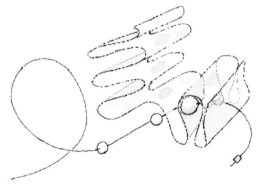

2 Cut a 50cm (20in) length of tiger tail and secure one end by pressing the crimp tube tightly in place (this is simply to prevent the pearls falling off as you thread them). Thread the tiger tail through the centre of the width of the net, add two small pearls, bring the net around and thread again with the tiger tail. Add a large pearl and thread the net again, followed by two smaller pearls. This creates a ruffle effect.

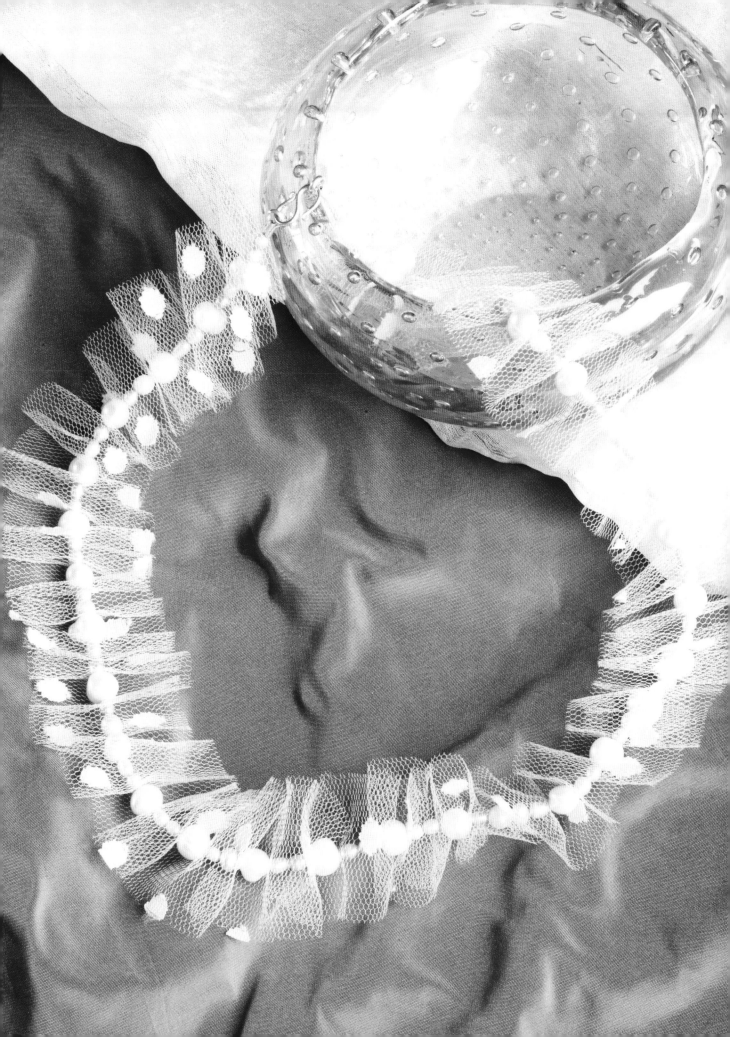

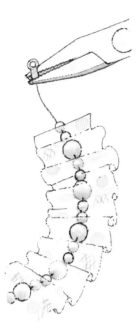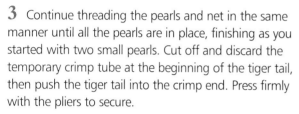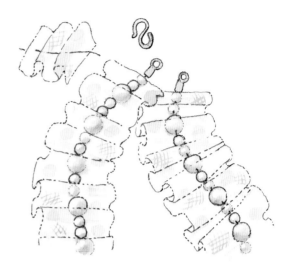

3 Continue threading the pearls and net in the same manner until all the pearls are in place, finishing as you started with two small pearls. Cut off and discard the temporary crimp tube at the beginning of the tiger tail, then push the tiger tail into the crimp end. Press firmly with the pliers to secure.

4 Push the pearls together and adjust the ruffle before cutting off the extra net and tiger tail at the other end, leaving just enough tiger tail to push into the crimp end. Add the second crimp end and press to secure. Attach the snake clasp through the ring on the crimp end (the necklace closes into the ring on the other crimp end).

Ruched ribbon earrings

The technique of threading beads
or semi-precious stones can be
adapted to a multitude of
decorative jewellery designs. The
subtly coloured ruched silk ribbon
gently encloses grey freshwater
pearls in these elegant and
unusual earrings. A matching
necklace has been made with grey
freshwater pearls interspersed with
small chips of moonstone.

Organdie Ribbon Necklace with Mother-of-Pearl Leaves

These shimmering mother-of-pearl leaves have been cut from an abalone shell and can be bought in long strands. These particular leaves have a single hole drilled at the top, allowing the narrowest of organdie ribbons to be threaded through. Each leaf is fixed in place along the length of the ribbon by single knots and all three strands of ribbon are brought together through a single pink glass bead at each end. Using three strands of ribbon in complementary colours means a generous number of leaves can be threaded, creating a sumptuous effect.

MATERIALS

1m (1 yard) lengths of organdie ribbon in cream, mauve and pink, 4mm (3/16in) wide

Needle (check it fits through the holes in the leaves)

36 mother-of-pearl leaves, drilled with holes

2 small pink glass beads

2 silver calottes

2 silver jump rings, 4mm (3/16in) and 6mm (1/4in) in diameter

1 silver snake clasp

Scissors

Flat-nosed pliers

Round-nosed pliers

White craft glue (optional)

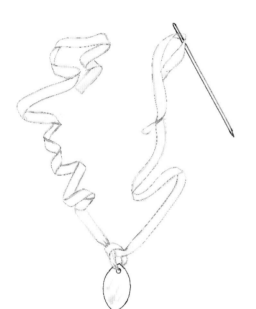

1 Thread the needle with the first length of ribbon, thread through the hole at the top of a leaf shape and tie the ribbon around in a single knot to hold in place roughly in the centre of the ribbon.

TIP

Choose your ribbon colours to echo and enhance the reflective tones of the mother-of-pearl leaves.

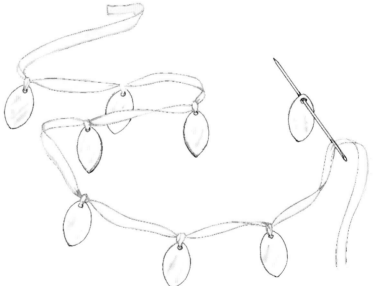

2 Tie on more leaves in the same way on either side of this central leaf, spacing them about 4cm (1½in) apart, until you have knotted 12 leaves in place.

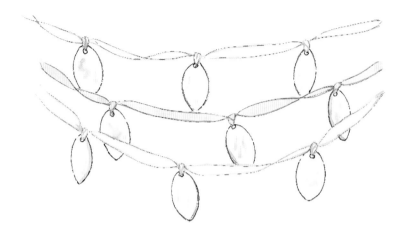

3 Repeat this same process on the other two lengths of ribbon, adjusting the width of the knots so that the leaves will appear evenly along the three ribbons when placed alongside each other.

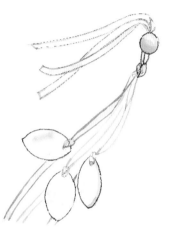

4 Bring the three lengths of ribbon together at the ends and tie into a knot, then thread the ends through one of the pink glass beads.

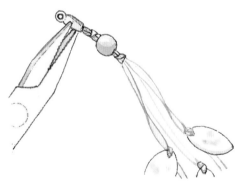

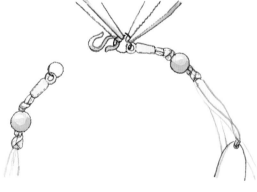

5 Tie another knot just after the pink bead and cut off the ribbons so that the ends just fit into the calotte. You can add a dab of glue here for extra security, if you wish. Close the calotte over the ribbon ends with the flat-nosed pliers.

6 Repeat with another pink bead and calotte on the other end of the necklace. Add the two jump rings to each of the rings on the calottes. Add the snake clasp to the smaller jump ring and close firmly using both pairs of pliers.

Buttons, pearl discs and tiny shells on silk ribbons

Small buttons, tiny shells and pearl discs have been simply tied
to three strands of blue-toned narrow silk ribbon to create this
exquisite and delicate necklace. Belying its appearance, silk is one of
the strongest textiles and so will support quite a range of materials
suspended from it. The three ribbons are knotted and secured
through the split ring and clasp using a silver crimp tube, and
a simple silver snake clasp finishes the necklace.

Copper and Metallic Organdie Bracelet

This pretty copper chain bracelet has no clasp – the technique is simply to make the chain circle large enough to slip over the wrist. A length of clear beading elastic has been threaded through the links and joined, pulling the chain in slightly so it won't slip off while being worn. This is a simple idea which avoids the need to attach a clasp. The shaped glass beads are easily attached using endpins and the finished bracelet is given a shimmering, lustrous quality by attaching short ties of copper-coloured metallic organdie.

MATERIALS

22cm (8½in) length of copper chain

Copper jump ring, 5mm (¼in) in diameter

8 copper endpins, 5cm (2in) in length

10 assorted pink/red shaped glass beads

Offcut of copper metallic organdie

40cm (16in) clear beading elastic, 0.8mm thick

1 gold-coloured crimp tube, 3mm (⅛in) in diameter

Sharp scissors

Flat-nosed pliers

Round-nosed pliers

Wirecutters

1 Join the length of chain together with the jump ring – you will need to use the two pairs of pliers, one to hold the ring while you close it with the other pair.

2 Thread the endpins through the glass beads (you can thread the smaller beads in pairs) and, using the round-nosed pliers, bend over the protruding wire to make the beginning of a loop. Attach the beads to the chain by threading this loop through the links, then turn the wire around on itself a couple of times and cut off the excess with the wirecutters. Attach the beads equidistantly around the chain.

3 Cut 20 lengths of the organdie, each measuring approximately 10cm (4in) long and 2cm (¾in) wide. Tie them in single knots evenly around the chain, through the individual links.

4 Thread the elastic through each link of the chain. Pull slightly to fit the wrist size and thread each end of the elastic through the opposite side of the crimp tube. Close the tube by pressing tightly with the flat-nosed pliers and cut off the excess ends.

Carved Bone Beads on Twisted Satin Cord and Black Braid

Black and white is a timeless and enduring combination in the fields of both fashion and design. In this elegant project, the black and white theme has been exploited by the use of carved natural bone beads. Carving bone is an ancient craft that has used this most readily available material from the earliest times. There are many intricate examples in museums, but these readily available modern Chinese beads are inexpensive to buy. Knotted and threaded onto the twisted satin cord and a contrasting black braid, they make a stylish piece of jewellery.

MATERIALS

1.5m (1½ yards) ivory twisted satin cord

1.5m (1½ yards) narrow black braid

Selection of carved bone beads in assorted shapes, 11 white and 11 black

1 bone button, 2.5cm (1in) in diameter

Scissors

White craft glue

1 Dab some glue onto the ends of the cord and braid. As it begins to dry, roll it and press the ends to make a firm end for threading. Tie a knot in the satin cord 17cm (6½in) from the end, thread on a patterned square black bead and tie a holding knot next to the bead. Tie a double knot on the black braid 15cm (6in) from the end, thread on a carved white bead and tie a similar double holding knot on the other side.

2 Bring the two cords together and tie into a joining knot. Continue threading in the same manner – black beads on the white cord and white beads on the black braid, knotting the two cords together after one bead is threaded onto each thread. Stagger the beads so that they do not sit alongside each other.

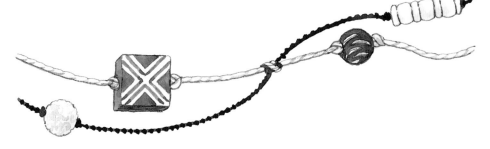

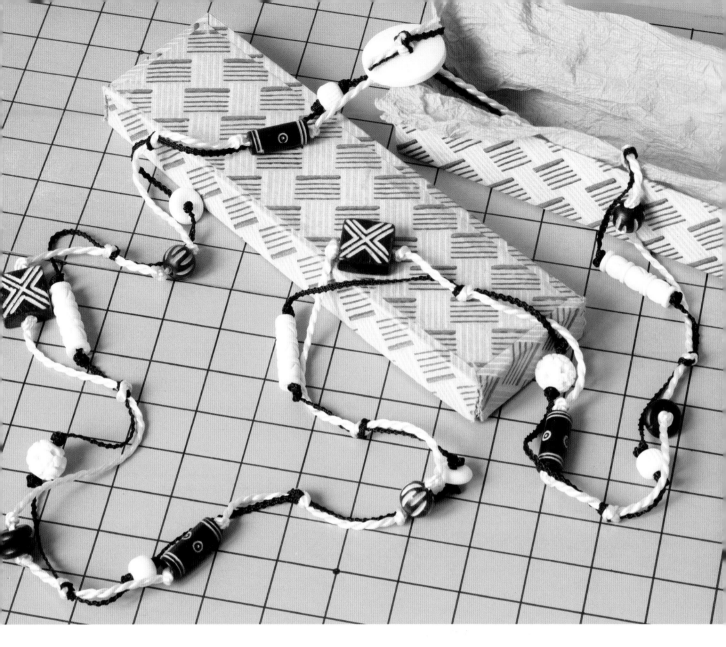

3 When you have knotted and threaded the necklace to the required length (the necklace here is 1m/1 yard long), tie each pair of cord/braid into a knot approximately 4cm (1½in) away from the last bead. Thread the two pairs of ends through separate holes in the bone button from the underside – you will now have four ends on the right side of the button.

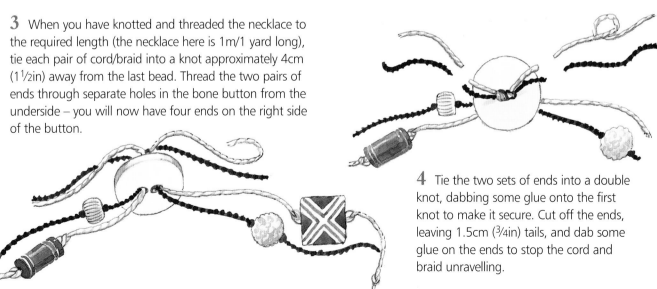

4 Tie the two sets of ends into a double knot, dabbing some glue onto the first knot to make it secure. Cut off the ends, leaving 1.5cm (¾in) tails, and dab some glue on the ends to stop the cord and braid unravelling.

Agate Pendant with Ribbon Rosette

This beautiful slice of agate with its internal contours makes a perfect pendant shape. Its stunning colours have been matched with an assortment of silk and rayon ribbons of different shades of purple and mauve. The addition of a rosette, created from a length of hand-dyed silk ribbon which has been cut on the cross, is not only decorative but also hides the hole and threading of the ribbons through the agate piece. Similarly, the four ribbons look beautiful but on a practical note, they are also stronger than a single ribbon.

MATERIALS

1m (1 yard) length of hand-dyed silk ribbon cut on the cross, 1.5cm (¾in) wide

Mauve thread

60cm (24in) length of purple-grey rayon ribbon, 1.5cm (¾in) wide

60cm (24in) length of lilac silk ribbon, 8mm (⅜in) wide

60cm (24in) length of mauve rayon ribbon, 7mm (⅜in) wide

10cm (4in) length of pale mauve narrow silk ribbon, 4mm (³⁄₁₆in) wide

Needle with large enough eye for the ribbon

Decorative vintage metal button

Slice of agate with drilled hole at one end

2 copper box calottes, 5mm (¼in)

2 copper jump rings, 5mm (¼in) in diameter

1 copper lobster clasp

Scissors

Round-nosed pliers

Flat-nosed pliers

White craft glue

1 Cut off 40cm (16in) of the hand-dyed silk ribbon and make a small rosette, each loop measuring 2cm (¾in). As you create the loops, sew them in place from behind with the mauve thread. Cut off the excess ribbon, fold over the end and stitch in place to finish.

2 Lay all the 60cm (24in) lengths of ribbon parallel. Thread the needle with the 10cm (4in) length of narrow silk ribbon. Hold the button in the centre of the front of the rosette and hold the four ribbons across the back. Thread the needle through the button, then through the hole in the back of the agate. Pass it over the four strands of ribbon, through the rosette and through one of the holes on the button on the front of the rosette. Bring the ribbon back through the other button hole, through the rosette once more, under the set of four ribbons and then out through the hole in the agate and the other hole in the button.

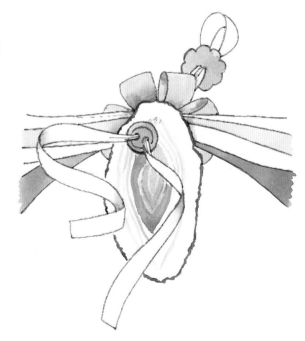

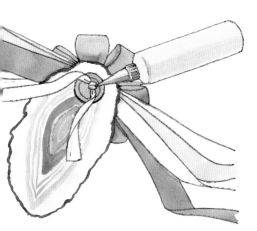

3 Pull the ribbon really tightly through all the layers to hold them in place, tie a single knot and dab a small amount of glue on the knot before tying again. Cut off the excess ends at 1cm (½in). You can smear a small amount of glue on the cut ends to prevent fraying. When dry, cut again through the glue to neaten the edge.

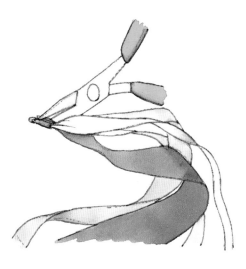

4 Cut the four ribbons on each side so they measure 22cm (8¾in). Fold all the ends together on one side so they fit neatly into the box calotte, hold in place with the round-nosed pliers whilst beginning to press the sides together with the flat-nosed pliers. When one side is pressed over slightly, remove the round-nosed pliers and continue pressing both sides firmly until the ribbon is held securely. To close the necklace, add a jump ring to each of the rings on the calottes using both pairs of pliers. Before closing the jump ring on one side, pass it through the small ring on the lobster clasp.

Silk Bows and Pink Glass Beads on Copper Chain

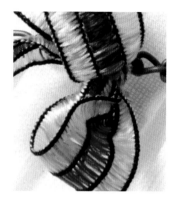

Breaking up a chain by the insertion of beads along its length is a common jewellery design technique, whereby the wire threaded through the bead becomes a sort of link in the chain. This delicate piece has the added effect of creating a pendant of three chains of varying lengths with bead ends. The unusual idea of tying pretty silk bows along the chain between the beads transforms this simple necklace into a really eye-catching piece of jewellery. You could even change the colour or texture of the bows to suit your outfit.

MATERIALS

1m (1 yard) copper or base metal chain

7 patterned oval pink glass beads

8 faceted pink glass beads

12 copper or base metal eyepins

3 copper or base metal endpins

Selection of narrow silk ribbon offcuts, such as pink, purple, rust, striped, etc

Scissors

Round-nosed pliers

Wirecutters

White craft glue

1 Use the wirecutters to cut the chain into 13 lengths each of nine links (you will need to discard the cut link). Also cut one short length of five links and one long length of 15 links.

2 Thread six of the oval beads and six of the faceted beads onto eyepins. Using round-nosed pliers, bend the protruding wire around into an open loop, then cut off the excess wire and thread the open loop through the last link of one of the medium lengths of chain. Bring the wire around and tuck it back into the hole in the top of the bead to hide and secure.

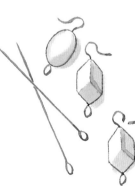

3 Add another medium length of chain to the ring at the base of the first bead, continue threading in this way, linking the two shapes of beads alternately onto the same length of chain until 11 beads are in place. Fold the beaded chain in half and the beads on each side should match.

4 Bring the two ends of the chain together and attach the loop on the remaining oval glass bead onto the two end links. This joins the chain and makes a central anchor bead on which to hang the three-chain pendant.

5 Use the round-nosed pliers to open out the ring at the base of the anchor bead. Thread this open loop through the three remaining chains of differing lengths. Thread the remaining three beads onto the three endpins and attach each one as before into the last link of each chain.

6 Tie an assortment of small ribbon bows midway between the beads through the central link in the chain. Leave six sections (the part that goes around the back of the neck) without bows. Add bows to the three chains at the base of the necklace, arranging them so they don't all bunch up together. This is a fiddly job and it is a good idea to tie the narrowest ribbons into double ties. Trim the ends neatly and seal with a smear of white glue.

Charm Bracelet with Woven Silk Ribbons

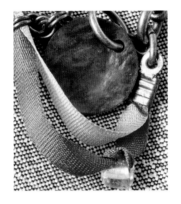

A charm bracelet is one of jewellery's great classics – it never goes out of fashion. This is partly because the charms are often mementoes or presents and thus have a personal significance, with many people collecting and adding to their charm bracelets over time. The silver and copper charms used here are readily found in specialist bead shops and are inexpensive to buy. The addition of the double silk ribbon, weaving itself through the links of the small copper chain, makes a conventional piece of jewellery really decorative and unusual.

MATERIALS

- 20cm (8in) length of small-link copper chain (or a size to fit comfortably around your wrist)
- 1 copper jump ring, 3mm (1/8in) in diameter
- 1 small copper lobster clasp
- 14 copper jump rings, 5mm (1/4in) in diameter
- 13 assorted charms, including 6 copper discs
- 2 small copper box calottes
- 2 oval jump rings, 3mm (1/8in) in diameter
- 40cm (16in) each pink and red narrow silk ribbon, 3mm (1/8in) wide
- 9 pink seed beads
- 2 needles with large eyes
- Flat-nosed pliers
- Round-nosed pliers
- Wirecutters
- White craft glue

1 Open out a small jump ring and link around the last link at one end of the chain, passing it through the small ring on the lobster clasp. Close tightly. It helps to hold the ring in place with one set of pliers whilst closing the ring with the others. Attach a large jump ring to the other end of the chain in the same manner.

TIP

The narrowest silk ribbon has been used here so it is important to find really small box calottes to hold the ribbon at both ends.

2 Open out the remaining larger jump rings. Beginning at one end, attach the charms along the length of the chain, making sure you close the jump rings firmly around the chosen links to keep the charms secure.

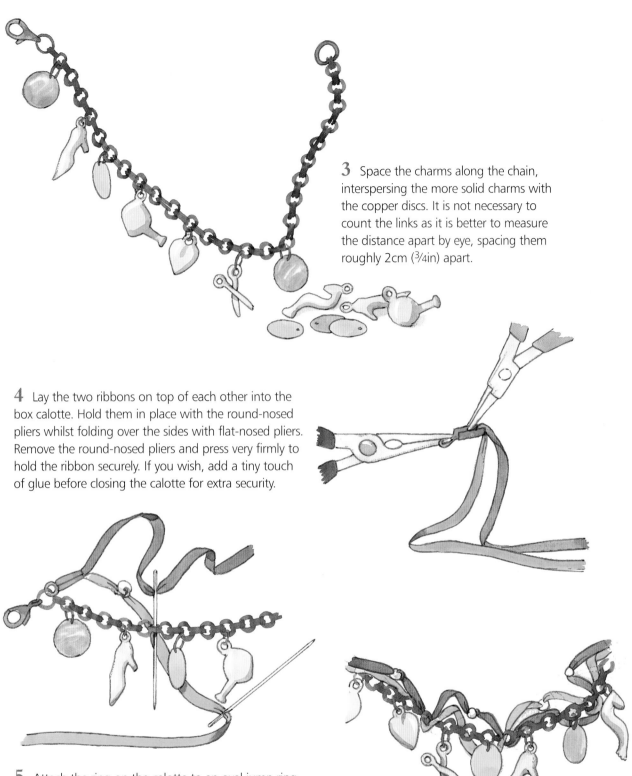

3 Space the charms along the chain, interspersing the more solid charms with the copper discs. It is not necessary to count the links as it is better to measure the distance apart by eye, spacing them roughly 2cm (³⁄₄in) apart.

4 Lay the two ribbons on top of each other into the box calotte. Hold them in place with the round-nosed pliers whilst folding over the sides with flat-nosed pliers. Remove the round-nosed pliers and press very firmly to hold the ribbon securely. If you wish, add a tiny touch of glue before closing the calotte for extra security.

5 Attach the ring on the calotte to an oval jump ring and, in turn, attach this to the jump ring at the end of the chain. Thread the silk ribbons through the two separate needles. Thread a seed bead onto the red ribbon and tie in place with a single knot. Thread both ribbons through the same link of the chain after the second charm. Now thread and tie another seed bead onto the pink ribbon.

6 Weave the ribbons loosely in and out of the chain between the charms, adding a seed bead alternately to the red or pink ribbon. When you reach the other end, finish by securing the two ribbons into a box calotte, pressing tightly as before to secure. Attach to the jump ring at the other end of the chain.

Moonstone Bracelet

Moonstone is a beautiful semi-precious stone. It appears to exude an almost magical silvery light, hence its name. To enhance this mysterious quality, it is important not to overwhelm the stone with strong colour or complicated design. Here the simple beads have been threaded and knotted onto a pale eau-de-nil narrow silk ribbon. Make sure that your intended beads have a central hole large enough for the needle and ribbon to pass through. You will need to adjust the length of your bracelet to fit. Here, a small button is used to finish the bracelet before the ribbon ends are tied into a decorative bow. This is a delightful project which would make a lovely present for a young girl.

MATERIALS

1m (1 yard) eau-de-nil silk ribbon, 8mm (3⁄8in) wide

Needle (with an eye large enough to thread the ribbon but small enough to fit through the bead hole)

27 moonstone beads, 5mm (1⁄4in) in diameter

1 pale blue button

Scissors

White craft glue

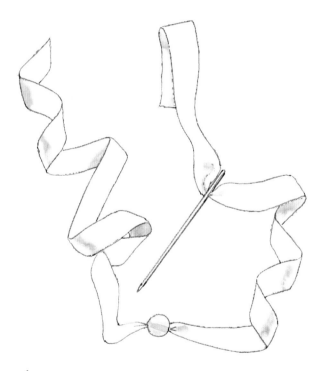

1 Thread the ribbon though the needle and pass a bead centrally onto the ribbon.

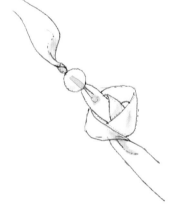

2 Tie a single knot in the ribbon on each side of the bead and close to it.

TIP

When knotting, you will need at least twice as much ribbon as the length of your necklace.

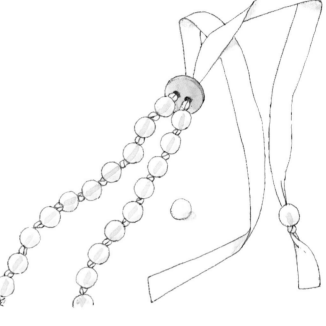

3 Continue threading the beads onto the ribbon either side of the central bead with tight knots against each bead until you have 25 in place. Make a final knot after each last bead at both ends.

4 Pass the two ribbon ends through the two holes in the button from behind. Thread one more bead on each ribbon end and make a final knot after these beads. Cut off the excess ribbon, leaving a 1cm (½in) tail. Add a smear of white glue along this edge to seal the edges, then, when dry, cut again to make a neat and unfrayed end. To fasten the bracelet, tie the ribbon ends into a secure bow.

Pink glass necklace with lilac and pink ribbons

This classic bead stringing technique can be applied to many kinds of beads. Using two ribbons in different shades makes the knots between the beads particularly decorative and narrow ribbons can be threaded through the eye of a needle together. The subtle pink colouring of the pressed glass beads used here works beautifully with the pink and lilac tones of the rayon ribbon.

Shell Pendant on Satin Ribbon

This stunning project is so simple to make. There is little technique involved as the effect of the piece relies on using materials of the best quality. All it takes is a bold and beautiful large polished shell, some freshwater pearls, a sumptuous satin ribbon and solid silver jump rings and clasp. The shell has the advantage of being able to be worn either way around – the concave side cradling the mother-of-pearl flower and the string of white freshwater pearls, or the reverse side displaying the simple natural beauty of the shell.

MATERIALS

1 small silver jump ring, 4mm (^{3}/16in) in diameter

1 mother-of-pearl flower

3 white freshwater pearls

1 silver endpin with decorated base

1m (1 yard) pale gold satin ribbon, 4cm (1^1/2in) wide

Natural polished shell, 7cm (2^3/4in) in diameter

1 large silver closed ring, 12mm (^{5}/8in) in diameter

2 silver closed rings, 10mm (^{1}/2in) in diameter

1 silver jump ring, 7mm (^{3}/8in) in diameter

1 silver snake clasp

Scissors

Round-nosed pliers

Flat-nosed pliers

Wirecutters

White craft glue

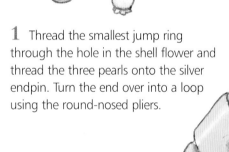

1 Thread the smallest jump ring through the hole in the shell flower and thread the three pearls onto the silver endpin. Turn the end over into a loop using the round-nosed pliers.

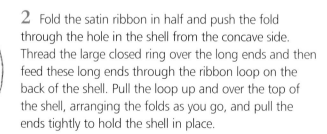

2 Fold the satin ribbon in half and push the fold through the hole in the shell from the concave side. Thread the large closed ring over the long ends and then feed these long ends through the ribbon loop on the back of the shell. Pull the loop up and over the top of the shell, arranging the folds as you go, and pull the ends tightly to hold the shell in place.

3 Attach the shell flower to the large silver ring around the ribbon by closing the jump ring. Feed the loop of the endpin holding the pearls over the same silver ring, bring it back on itself and twist around the stem a couple of times using the flat-nosed pliers. Cut off the excess wire using the wirecutters.

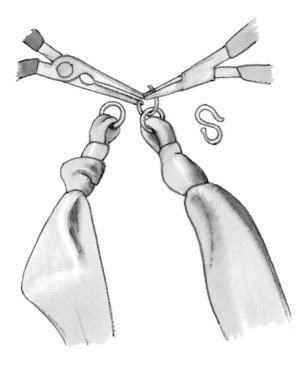

4 Thread the end of the ribbon through the 1cm (½in) closed ring and tie the ribbon into a knot approximately 20cm (8in) from the loop around the shell. Cut off the end of the ribbon at 2cm (¾in) and tuck out of sight behind the knot and in the gathering of the ribbon, smearing a small dab of glue along the cut edge of ribbon to prevent fraying. Repeat on the other side, this time attaching the 7mm (⅜in) jump ring to the large silver ring enclosed in the ribbon. Attach the snake clasp to the single ring to close.

4 buttons and beads

There has been a real revival in the use of buttons as important elements in fashion and more recently this has spread to their use in jewellery design. Almost anything is available – natural materials include bone, stone, shell, pearl, horn and wood. Then there are the wonderful buttons made from glass, plastic, Bakelite or metal, or those inset with precious stones. Buttons have a fascinating history and there are museums dedicated to them. The fact that buttons are usually drilled through with two or four holes means they are eminently suitable for threading, and they work beautifully in contrast or conjunction with other elements. Ribbons in particular look really good weaving in and out of the central hole, as shown in several projects in this chapter.

Multi-coloured Silk Ribbon Bracelet with Pearl Buttons

This brightly coloured ribbon bracelet features shaped mother-of-pearl buttons threaded together with six strands of narrow silk ribbon. The vibrant shades of the ribbon give the bracelet a fun, summery appearance, but the design would work equally well using muted shades of grey and silver ribbon, producing a more sophisticated piece of jewellery. No clasp has been used here; instead, a button is cleverly used to slide along the ribbons, allowing you to adjust the size of the bracelet. A cross-grained rayon ribbon has been threaded through similar buttons for the bracelet shown on the right of the photograph. In both designs, the bracelets have been finished by knotting the ribbon ends after threading through additional buttons.

1 Thread the needle with all six ribbons. Take the needle through the first hole of the button from the underside. Bring the needle back through the second hole, then slide the button along the ribbons until it sits in the centre of them.

MATERIALS

Chenille needle

50cm (20in) lengths of light and dark pink, orange, yellow, maroon and red silk ribbon, 3mm (1/8in) wide

8 mother-of-pearl buttons with two holes, some preferably in unusual shapes

Scissors

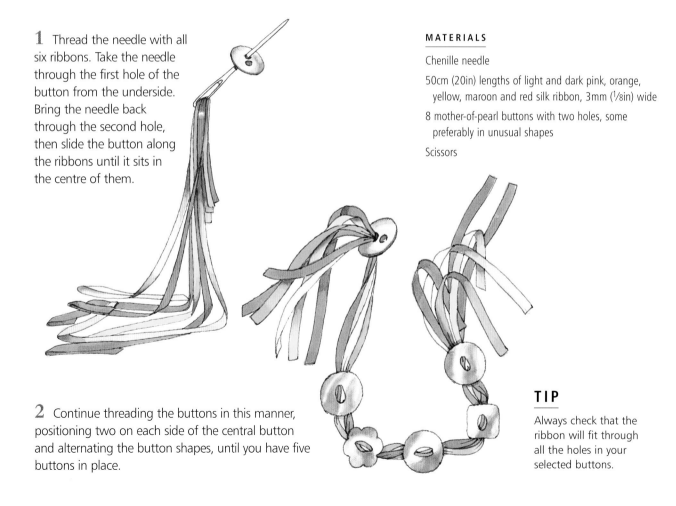

2 Continue threading the buttons in this manner, positioning two on each side of the central button and alternating the button shapes, until you have five buttons in place.

TIP

Always check that the ribbon will fit through all the holes in your selected buttons.

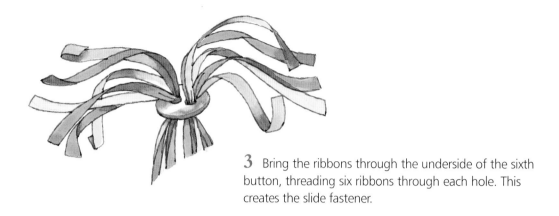

3 Bring the ribbons through the underside of the sixth button, threading six ribbons through each hole. This creates the slide fastener.

4 Cut the ribbon ends to leave tails of 7.5cm (3in), then thread another button onto the ends. Tie each bundle of ribbons into a neat single knot to hold this button in place and cut off the ends to leave 2cm (¾in) remaining.

Blue chiffon ribbon bracelet with pearl buttons and drop beads

This charming bracelet is so simple to make. A single length of narrow chiffon ribbon has been carefully threaded through the smoky-toned mother-of-pearl buttons. The button slide fastener means there is no need to use a more conventional metal clasp. The design is enhanced by the use of pretty drop beads spaced between the buttons. This simple technique can easily be adapted to make a larger piece of jewellery, such as a matching necklace – just remember to select buttons with holes of a suitable size to accommodate the width of ribbon.

Pink Pompom Necklace

This stunning necklace with its random assortment of cotton pompoms, beads, buttons and flowers on silk and satin ribbon and silk thread is a real statement in pink! Although it looks complicated, there are really no rules and each person will string this necklace differently. It is a wonderful project for using up an assortment of materials leftover after making other pieces of jewellery. The only thing to remember is to bring the ribbons together periodically in twos or threes into a knot between the threading of all the decorative elements.

MATERIALS

1.5m (1½ yards) pink silk pearl stringing thread, with threader attached

1.5m (1½ yards) brick red silk ribbon, 4mm (³/₁₆in) wide

1.5m (1½ yards) fuschia satin ribbon, 1cm (½in) wide

Needle with eye large enough to take the narrow silk ribbon

Selection of assorted beads, such as wooden beads, glass seed beads, shaped beads, etc

14 pink, red and orange buttons in a variety of sizes

5 assorted silk flowers

Pink cotton pompoms, cut from braid

Scissors

White craft glue

1 Lay all three lengths of ribbon/thread together and tie all three into a knot 12cm (4¾in) from one end (the threader on the pearl stringing thread should be at the other end). Thread the narrow silk ribbon into the needle. Thread a pink wooden bead onto the pink thread, followed by a small orange button and tie a double knot after the button. Thread the satin and silk ribbons together through the square wooden bead, separate them and thread the satin ribbon through a pink button so that it lies flat.

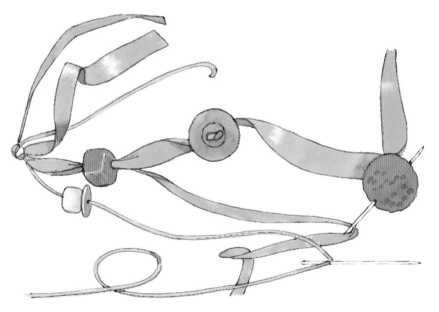

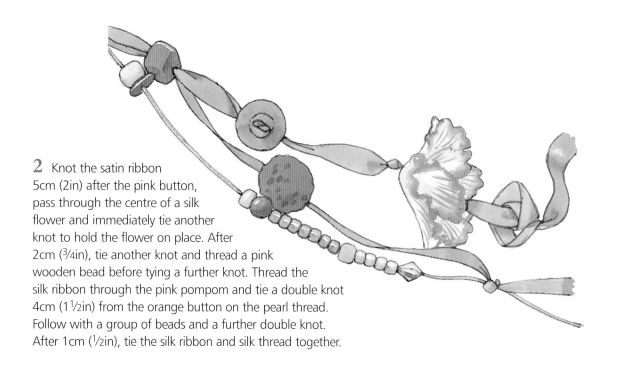

2 Knot the satin ribbon 5cm (2in) after the pink button, pass through the centre of a silk flower and immediately tie another knot to hold the flower on place. After 2cm (¾in), tie another knot and thread a pink wooden bead before tying a further knot. Thread the silk ribbon through the pink pompom and tie a double knot 4cm (1½in) from the orange button on the pearl thread. Follow with a group of beads and a further double knot. After 1cm (½in), tie the silk ribbon and silk thread together.

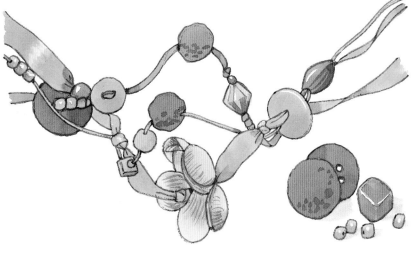

3 Continue threading the necklace in a random fashion with the flowers, larger beads and buttons on the satin ribbon, the cotton pompoms and smaller buttons on the silk ribbon, and the smallest beads and buttons on the silk thread. Periodically bring these threads together in a knot to give cohesion to the necklace.

4 When the necklace is 1m (1 yard) long, finish off by tying the three cords into a knot at each end, pass the two sets of ends through the two holes on a larger pink button from underneath. Tie them together on the right side of the button, add a dab of glue and tie a second knot. Trim the ends and smear some glue along the cut. When dry, cut neatly again to prevent fraying.

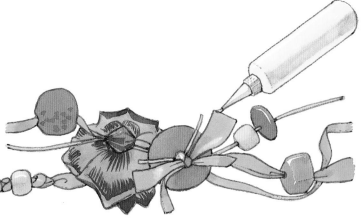

Pink pompoms, buttons and beads

This simpler necklace with its ribbon-tie
ends uses similar elements in a more
economical way. The pretty selection of
beads, buttons and three sorts of cotton
pompoms has been randomly threaded
onto pale pink satin rat tail and a yellow
pearl threading silk. This kind of necklace
is an ideal project for using up spare
beads and leftover threads.

Abalone Button Bracelet

The pearly iridescence of the polished abalone shell has a magical property. It is one of the most extraordinary materials from the natural world, and as such has been prized for its rich decorative quality. It has many applications, including inlay in furniture (which was popular in the nineteenth century) and particularly its use in jewellery design. These buttons with the wonderfully deep tones come from New Zealand, where for generations this exquisite shell has been used in the art and craft of the Maori people.

MATERIALS

1m (1 yard) dip-dyed chiffon ribbon, 3cm (1¼in) wide
6 abalone buttons, 3cm (1¼in) in diameter
Tapestry needle
White craft glue

1 Fold the ribbon in half and tie a knot at the fold end to create a 3cm (1¼in) loop.

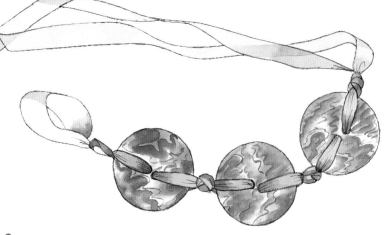

2 Push the first button up against the knot between the two strands of ribbon. Bring one end behind the button and through the second hole; take the other strand of ribbon over the front of the button and through the first hole.

3 After the first button, tie the two ends of the ribbon into a single knot. Add another button, threading the two ends as before and tying a knot immediately after.

TIP

It helps to push the ribbon through the hole with the eye of a needle.

4 Continue threading in this manner until five buttons are in place, then tie another knot and add the last button. Instead of tying a knot after it, bring one end of the ribbon around the edge of the button towards the hole where the other ribbon emerges. Tie the ribbon tightly at this point into a double knot, adding a touch of glue after the first knot to secure. Cut off the excess ribbon ends so they are hidden by the button.

Vintage Shirt Button Necklace

These unremarkable, utilitarian white shirt buttons have been recovered from an inherited button box. There was a time when buttons would always have been retrieved when clothes were worn out, to be used on another garment. These vintage buttons have waited a long time but when rediscovered, their simple qualities helped design this rather clever, modern-looking necklace. It is incredibly straightforward to make – the pink and white ribbons are simply woven through the holes in the buttons and beads. As there are four holes in each button and the ribbons pass through the same hole, this has the effect of making the buttons sit deliberately off-centre.

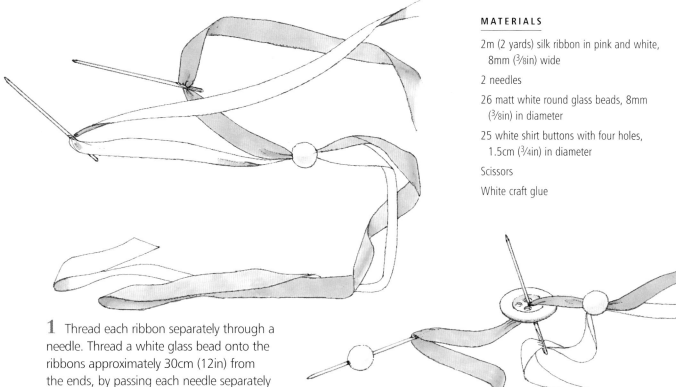

MATERIALS

2m (2 yards) silk ribbon in pink and white, 8mm (³⁄₈in) wide

2 needles

26 matt white round glass beads, 8mm (³⁄₈in) in diameter

25 white shirt buttons with four holes, 1.5cm (³⁄₄in) in diameter

Scissors

White craft glue

1 Thread each ribbon separately through a needle. Thread a white glass bead onto the ribbons approximately 30cm (12in) from the ends, by passing each needle separately through the hole in the bead. You will need to pull the ribbon tightly against the side of the bead hole in order to thread the second ribbon through.

2 Add a button next to the bead on the long side of the ribbons. Do this by passing the pink ribbon over and through a hole in the button whilst passing the white ribbon through the same hole from underneath the button. Now bring the two ribbons together, white on top and pink beneath, and pass the two ends through another glass bead.

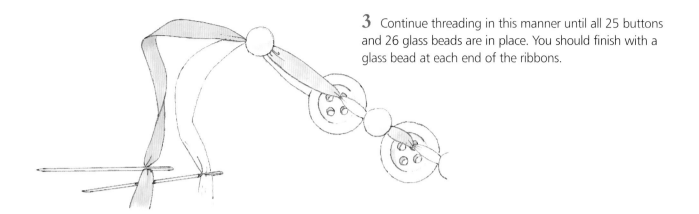

3 Continue threading in this manner until all 25 buttons and 26 glass beads are in place. You should finish with a glass bead at each end of the ribbons.

4 After the last bead, tie the two ribbons into a knot, leaving tails long enough (about 25cm/10in) to tie into a fastening bow. Add a smear of white glue to the ribbon ends to seal the threads; when dry, cut the ends neatly on a slant.

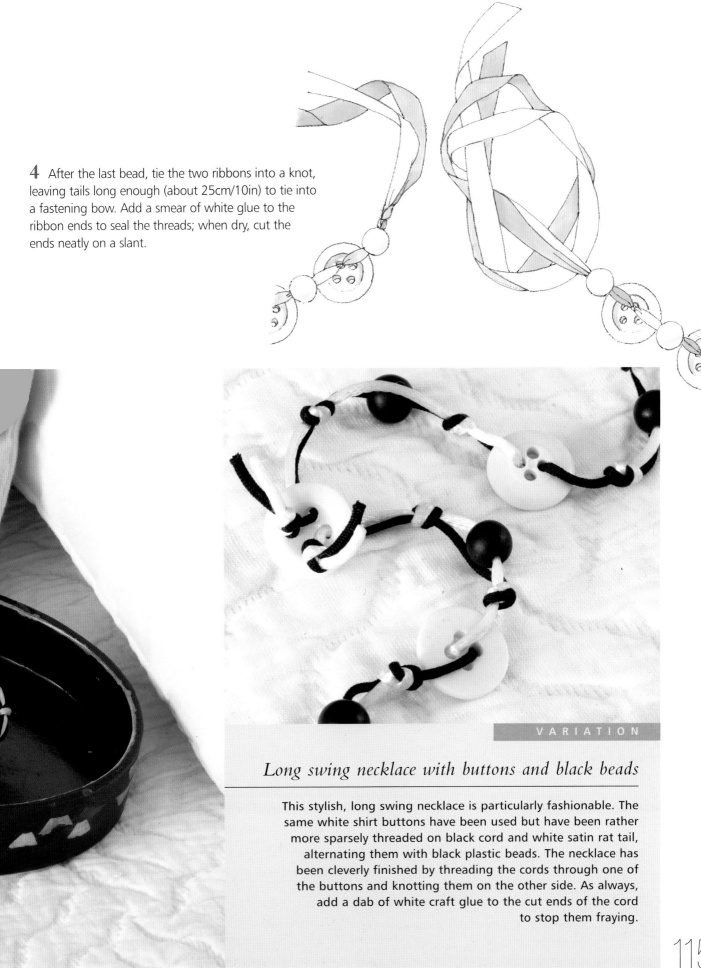

Long swing necklace with buttons and black beads

This stylish, long swing necklace is particularly fashionable. The same white shirt buttons have been used but have been rather more sparsely threaded on black cord and white satin rat tail, alternating them with black plastic beads. The necklace has been cleverly finished by threading the cords through one of the buttons and knotting them on the other side. As always, add a dab of white craft glue to the cut ends of the cord to stop them fraying.

Linen Heart Brooch

These charming little patchwork hearts are made from the smallest scraps of linen and are reminiscent of a lavender bag to secrete in your linen drawer. The indigo blue heart with its rust-coloured silk ribbon stitching has a small brooch pin sewn onto the back. The simplest decoration has been added in the form of a cross-grain ribbon bow with a vintage button accent. All the sewing has been done using a narrow silk ribbon as the thread. A small amount of cotton or polyester wadding has been added to give it a gently padded effect.

1 Fold the piece of paper in half and draw half a heart, butting up to the fold line of the paper. Cut out the heart and open up (it will form a complete, symmetrical heart). Pin the paper heart to a double thickness of linen. Cut neatly around the paper heart.

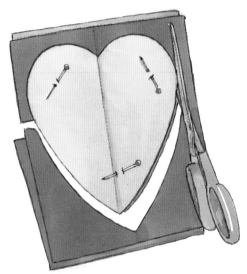

MATERIALS

Paper and pencil

Pins

Small scraps of indigo-dyed lightweight linen

20cm (8in) length of brown cross-grain ribbon

Needle with large eye

40cm (16in) length of brown narrow silk ribbon, 4mm ($^{3}/_{16}$in) wide

1 decorated brown vintage button

Small quantity of cotton or polyester wadding

1 brooch pin

Scissors

2 Working on one thickness of the fabric, take the cross-grain ribbon and arrange into three loops and two tails. Thread the needle with the narrow silk ribbon, bring the ribbon from behind, through the cross-grain bow and through the underside of the button. Then bring the ribbon through another hole on the front of the ribbon, back through the ribbon bow and through to the back. Come through once more so that the button is held by a crossed silk ribbon through the four holes in the button. Tie the ribbon in a double knot on the reverse to secure.

3 Sew the two sides of the heart together using the narrow silk ribbon in a running stitch 5mm ($^{1}/_{4}$in) in from the edge of the heart. Leave a 2cm ($^{3}/_{4}$in) gap on one side before finishing.

Silk flower heart

Once you have made one of these hearts you will want to experiment with different colours, fabrics and styles of decoration. The pink heart is decorated by sewing a button into the petals of a silk flower on top of a hand-dyed silk ribbon bow. The amounts of fabric used are so small and they are so quick to make that they would make sweet little presents, perhaps for a children's party.

4 Push the wadding into this gap (a pencil is useful for pushing the wadding into the corners) until the heart is loosely packed. Sew up the gap, finish off neatly on the wrong side and hide the end in the 'hem'. Finally, sew the brooch pin to the back using the same silk ribbon.

Colourful Button and Bead Necklace

This colourful necklace is simple to make and ideal for all those buttons and beads leftover from other projects. Flexible waxed cord has been threaded with an assortment of green, pink and red seed beads, punctuated with shaped beads and small buttons. Larger buttons have been strung on a green silk ribbon which weaves in and out and alongside the seed beads. As with many projects in this book, there is no need for complicated fastenings. When a necklace is long enough to fit over the head, hidden or decorative knots are easy and appropriate.

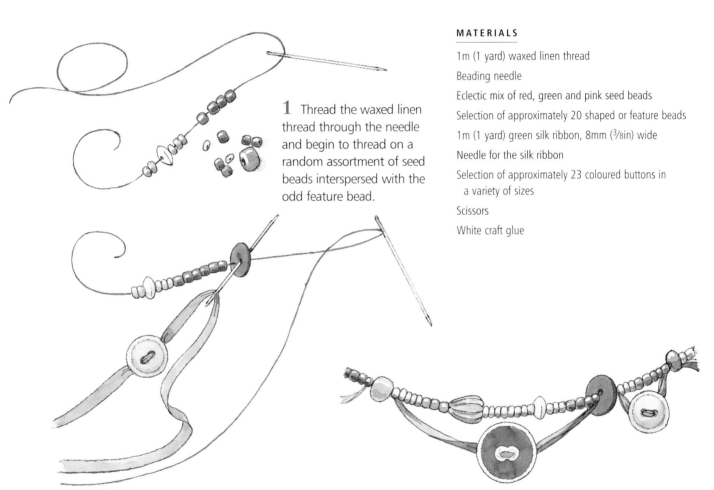

1 Thread the waxed linen thread through the needle and begin to thread on a random assortment of seed beads interspersed with the odd feature bead.

MATERIALS

1m (1 yard) waxed linen thread

Beading needle

Eclectic mix of red, green and pink seed beads

Selection of approximately 20 shaped or feature beads

1m (1 yard) green silk ribbon, 8mm (³⁄₈in) wide

Needle for the silk ribbon

Selection of approximately 23 coloured buttons in a variety of sizes

Scissors

White craft glue

2 Thread the green silk ribbon through the other needle and thread one of the larger buttons into the centre. Add a smaller button onto the beaded thread and pass the ribbon through the same button. On the opposite end, thread the ribbon through the larger feature bead, leaving the button to hang loosely on the ribbon.

3 Continue threading the necklace in this random manner, with beads on the thread and larger buttons along the ribbon.

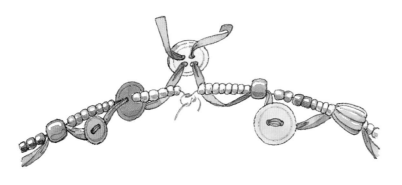

4 When the necklace has grown to a suitable length, thread the two ends of the silk through a four-hole button from the wrong side. Bring the ribbons back through the other holes and tie in a double knot, secured with a dab of white glue after the first knot. Cut off the excess ribbon, sealing the ends with a smear of white glue. At the same time, tie the thread with a double knot and hide the ends under adjoining beads.

Multi-strand Chiffon Ribbon Necklace

This exquisite shimmering piece of jewellery is deceptively simple to make, if a little time-consuming. Eight strands of translucent shot chiffon ribbon in different colours have been threaded with tiny iridescent seed beads. The green-gold button accents are simply tied around the beaded ribbons, gathering them together to make delicate swags. The lightness of the tiny beads makes them appear to float on the narrow chiffon and consequently the necklace sits beautifully around the neck.

MATERIALS

Beading needle, with eye large enough to take ribbon

1.5m (1½ yards) lengths of chiffon ribbon in 8 different colours, 5mm (¼in) wide, plus an extra 10cm (4in) length in any one colour

Selection of seed beads in yellow, pink, blue, orange, red, etc, 2mm (¹⁄₁₆in) in diameter

2 yellow foil-lined beads, 8mm (³⁄₈in) in diameter

2 extra-large gold-coloured crimp tubes (large enough to accommodate 16 ribbons)

1 snake clasp

2 gold-coloured split rings, 8mm (³⁄₈in) in diameter

7 green-gold pearl buttons, 12mm (⁵⁄₈in) in diameter

Scissors

Flat-nosed pliers

Beading glue

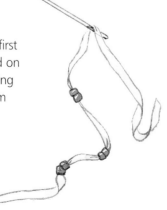

1 Thread the needle with the first length of chiffon ribbon. Thread on 80 identical seed beads, arranging them in pairs approximately 2cm (³⁄₄in) apart.

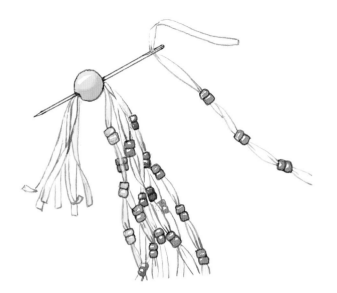

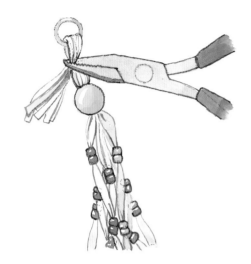

2 Thread the other seven strands of ribbon in the same way, changing the colour of seed beads on each different colour of ribbon. Bring all the threaded strands together at one end and pass them through the larger yellow bead. You will need to take each ribbon through individually with a needle.

3 Take the eight ribbons through the large crimp tube and around the split ring. Bring the ribbons back through the crimp tube once more. You may have to push them through individually with the eye end of the needle. Pull through enough to push and hide the ends in the yellow bead. Press the crimp to secure the ribbons using the flat-nosed pliers. Add a dab of beading glue inside the yellow bead and push in the ribbon ends to secure.

4 The necklace should measure about 50cm (20in) between the yellow beads. Add the snake clasp to the split ring at one end. Thread the short length of ribbon through the two holes on the right side of a button, approximately 5cm (2in) from one end gather the eight strands together and tie the ribbon and button around tightly, add a dab of glue on the knot, trim ends so they are hidden. Add all the other buttons along the necklace, roughly 5cm (2in) apart, facing the same way.

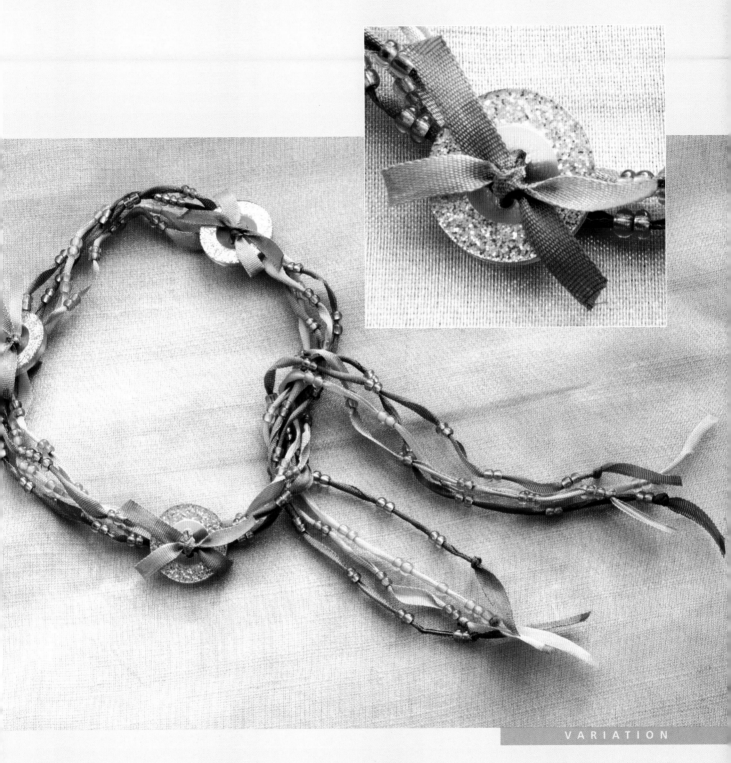

Tie bracelet

Four lengths of narrow silk ribbon have been used to make this simple tie bracelet. There is no fastening
as it is worn by tying the ends into a loose single or double knot. Using silk ribbon means that the
beads hang more heavily and do not float as they do when using chiffon ribbon. As always, you need to
match the width of the ribbon with the size of the central bead hole as well as the eye of the needle.

Stone Buttons on Suede and Linen Thread

Look closely at the stone disc buttons used for this necklace – they contain masses of tiny fossils. You may need to search around to find such lovely buttons, but you'll be amazed at the variety available. At one time all buttons were solely made from natural materials, such as stone, wood, horn or bone. They are still made from these sources today and are relatively inexpensive to buy. A natural material such as stone needs to be threaded with an equally natural material, and here the linen thread and suede thong complement the subtle colours in the stone.

1 Lay the suede and linen parallel and tie them together in a knot 35cm (14in) from one end. Cut the suede thong at an angle for easy threading and add a touch of glue to the linen thread to stop it unravelling. Thread a glass bead on the two strands from the long ends, separate the threads and take the suede thong over the front of the button and through the first hole. Bring the linen thread under the button and back through the second hole of the button.

2 Add another bead onto the double strands of suede and linen, then open out and thread another button in place. Continue threading in this manner (with a bead between each button) until nine buttons are in place. Add one more bead and tie a knot closely against it to hold all the buttons in place.

3 Working at one end, tie another knot 3cm (1¼in) from the last bead, thread another bead and after another 3cm (1¼in) tie another knot. After this knot add one last bead. Repeat this pattern on the other end of the necklace.

4 To make a sliding knot, lay the two sets of threads/thongs alongside each other. Turn one pair into a circle around the other pair, bring them around the back and through the circle, pull to tighten to make the knot. Repeat on the other side. The gap between the sliding knots should be approximately 10cm (4in). Cut the ends to 7cm (2¾in), thread on a last glass bead and tie a holding knot in the end. Cut off the excess to leave tails of 1cm (½in).

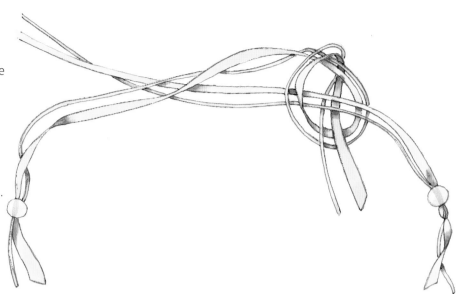

Stone buttons with suede and linen cord threading

The beautiful polished bone buttons used here have been threaded and knotted onto a spring-green suede thong. When you have strong elements such as texture, form and colour, sometimes it is a good idea to use them in a simple, restrained way for the best effect.

suppliers and acknowledgements

SUPPLIERS

Bead Aura
3 Neals Yard
Covent Garden
London WC2H 9DP
Tel: 020 7836 3002

www.beadaura.co.uk

Bead Shop
21A Tower Street
London WC2H 9NS
Tel: 020 7240 0931

www.beadshop.co.uk

Bijoux Beads
Elton House
2 Abbey Street
Bath BA1 1NN

Tel: 01225 482024

Swans Yard Craft Centre
High Street
Shaftesbury
Dorset SP7 8JQ
Tel: 01747 855688

www.bijouxbeads.co.uk

Celestial Trimmings
162 Archway Road
London N6 5BB
Tel: 020 8341 2788

London Bead Company/ Delicate Stitches
339 Kentish Town Road
London NW5 2TJ
Tel: 0870 203 2323

www.londonbeadco.co.uk

VV Rouleaux
6 Marylebone High Street
London W1M 3PB
Tel: 020 7224 5179

94 Miller Street
Merchant City
Glasgow G1 1DT
Tel: 0141 221 2277

38 Brentwood Avenue
Jesmond
Newcastle upon Tyne NE2 3DH
Tel: 0191 281 8338

www.vvrouleaux.com

Useful websites
www.beadaddict.co.uk
www.spangles4beads.co.uk
www.africantradebeads.com
www.orientaltrading.com
www.dressitupbuttonsandtrim.com
www.josyrose.co.uk

ACKNOWLEDGEMENTS

I would like to thank my husband Heini Schneebeli for taking the brilliant photographs in this book. I really appreciate the lovely step-by-step drawings by Kate Simunek. A big thank you to my publisher Cindy Richards for taking on my ideas and commissioning this book, and lastly as ever, so many thanks to my editor Gillian Haslam for her soothing influence, calm advice and seamless editing.

index